OTEQUE

TO SEU NATO,
DONA HELENA,
GUI E BER

ALBERTO LANDGRAF
WITH ANDREA PETRINI AND
ROBERT ASTLEY-SPARKE

# OTEQUE

IDEAS, PRINCIPLES, RECIPES,
STORIES AND CONNECTIONS

# OTEQUE MEANS “PLACE” IN LATIN…

**— Dr. Paulo Niemeyer, ABL Member**

From there come words like *biblioteca* (place of books), *enoteca* (place of wines), or even *discoteca* (place of dancing). By analogy, the restaurant Oteque, my favourite, could be called “otecaelum”, that is, “place near heaven”, because that’s how I feel when I’m there!

Jokes – though true – aside, let’s get to the point.

My relationship with Alberto Landgraf began for professional reasons – I was the doctor, he the patient – and over the years it turned into a friendship. That’s why I’m a firsthand (and first-palate) witness to the “Oteque Style”, and was even before its official opening in February 2018. I can assure you that from the very beginning, the divine and unique food, the original wine selection, the impeccable service, and the sophisticated yet relaxed atmosphere that sets it apart have always been hallmarks of the house.

Therefore, writing a few lines about this wonderful book that reveals the “Oteque Universe” is not only an honour but also an exercise in revisiting the most delicious memories.

Landgraf, who conceived the restaurant, is a landmark figure in global gastronomy – a consequence of the traits that define his personality. Cultured and educated well beyond the stove that brought him fame, “the Thinking Chef”, as he is often called, is above all a curious soul who loves to delve deeply into whatever catches his attention. His book is a reflection of all this.

Instructive, engaging and delightful to read, his book is accessible and fascinating, even for a layperson like me, because the gastronomy he describes is the result of years of experience and near-archaeological research into ancestral indigenous habits, culinary traditions of popular communities, curiosities from great tables around the world, and memories of family dishes – all blended with high technology and innovation. After all, he is the son of a Japanese mother and a German father, two cultures who exemplarily cultivate, revere and blend tradition with future. I’ve learned so much here!

And the great joy: Alberto gives us the illusion of “partnership” as he walks us through the pages of the book, telling his story, his experiences with renowned chefs he worked with, and even their “state secrets” (and pot secrets) – and his own too. Because of all this, and thanks to the simplicity that defines his storytelling, we’re left with the feeling that maybe one day we too will shine at our own four-burner stove.

Read it to believe it!

581
OTEQUE

# BLOOD IS THICKER THAN WATER

— **Alberto Landgraf**

I learned this saying from a chef I used to spend a lot of time with. It's a bold and strong statement. He often used this expression to describe how powerful family bonds are, or are meant to be, that at some point this connection will inevitably manifest itself. How does this relate to me and this book? I'll get back to that later.

The first cookbook I owned was *A Chef for All Seasons* by Gordon Ramsay, and I was stunned. I bought it the year it was published, in 2000, and I had barely started cooking professionally. Books in general always stunned me – my mother, a literature teacher, has instilled the passion for books in me since I was a little boy, so when I discovered that universe of cookbooks within the universe I had chosen as a profession – one that supposedly I would carry on for the rest of my life – I was in awe. When I was working in restaurants in Europe, I spent most of my days off in bookshops, leafing through different books and making notes, and never in my wildest dreams imagined that one day I would write a cookbook of my own.

Obviously, a lot has changed since those early days. I continued cooking, returned to Brazil, then had a few really bad jobs until I opened my first restaurant, Epice, in São Paulo in 2011, where I stayed until the end of 2015. Then came Oteque, which I opened in the beautiful city of Rio de Janeiro in March 2018. Now, I have the opportunity to share my thoughts and crazy ideas with you all in my own book. Next step: planting a tree.

**Principles**

It might seem strange at first, but there's a very simple line of thought as to why the chapters of this book are divided as they are: acidity, textures, blocks, leadership and creative process. I wanted the book to reflect the way I see food and cooking in a professional environment. You might be used to a more conventional cookbook structure, but I really didn't want to be "more of the same".

**Acidity** for me is key to (my) cooking – sharpness, always keeping the eater on the edge, all senses made alert by that electric zing. **Texture** is the fun of it all, a new discovery with every bite, contrasting always to bring balance. **Blocks** is the theory of life. From a Lego toy to childhood memories lingering in your subconscious, the whole universe is built by little blocks moving from here to there, so why not in cookery? **Leadership** and salt are two ingredients a kitchen can't do without. I always say that the difference between great food and bad food often can be about just a pinch of salt, and so it is with leadership. **Creative Process** is the most personal part of this book. It's where I share my approach to constructing the food that is served to guests at Oteque, the part that young cooks absorb and inherit when they work in my kitchen (and read this book).

The main reason I've written this book is to leave something for – and share something with – younger generations of chefs and cooks who can use it as a resource, to inspire them and help them in their careers.

**Being Carioca and The Mata Atlântica**

There's no way of living in Rio de Janeiro and not being aware of and absorbing the "carioca" lifestyle. Easygoing and laid back, Rio and its people have a lot of swagger, and you'll always find someone up for a chat (the famous *resenha*). It's a place where clocks don't work like anywhere else – there's always gonna be something to do, and someone willing to do it with you. This is truly a place that never sleeps.

But, spend time in the city and you also get to know about the sadness in its past. Rio was the capital of Brazil during the empire, where the royal family held court, and the ugly heritage of slavery still lingers around us. Although we can still contemplate the city's beauty, especially driving south through the *Serra do Mar* – in places like Angra, Paraty and many small villages like Ponta Negra, where many of the landscape and nature photographs in this book were taken – nature and humanity coexist in ways that Robert's beautiful photography in this book manages to capture with justice.

The data varies, but it is believed that only about 10 per cent of the Atlantic rainforest – the Mata Atlântica – remains intact. Without getting myself into hot water here, I believe this situation is infinitely worse than what's happening in the Amazon, though it doesn't carry the same marketing appeal. Chefs who live in and make their living from the devastated Mata Atlântica should care and do more for the natives and local communities, rather than use the Amazon and Amazonian cuisine as a cheap marketing tool to promote their work.

**Carbon Footprint**

I met Ricardo Vicario and Alberto Colombo from REACH EAT when they were just a startup with a dream: to help the food industry understand and reduce its carbon footprint. I strongly suggested they focus on fine dining restaurants first, and I think it worked. This book provides the proof: all the dishes within these pages have had their carbon footprints meticulously calculated, and the data is there for all to see.

It's a bold step toward culinary sustainability. Alberto and Ricardo now run REACH EAT, a London-based company that empowers chefs, food producers and consumers to make informed, climate-conscious decisions. Their mission – to make sustainability measurable, actionable and accessible – aligns perfectly with the values behind this book.

**London, Japan, Blood**

Through many talks with my brother, a dedicated biologist, about the Mata Atlântica, I came to know fruits, ingredients, herbs and mushrooms I'd never imagined were edible. But more than that, I learned how to value and pay attention to the people behind the hard work. We chefs work hard, but the hardest work in the chain is far from ours – it belongs to the producers who work the land, the fishers who sail the boats, the butchers who prepare the meat. They are the ones who truly keep the wheels turning.

As a young chef learning the trade in London, I remember asking the chefs to arrange work for me on my days off – at the butcher's, or at the fishmonger's – just so I could learn more. I ended up getting my NVQ qualification at Westminster Kingsway College. London is where I began working as a young chef, as a young adult, and I still carry a deep, meaningful connection to the city today. Without London in my life, I wouldn't be here writing these crazy words to you.

Now, to explain the title of this introduction. Once, in a casual conversation, a renowned chef told me that the moment that would change my life would be my first trip to Japan – that it had changed many chefs' lives but that it would likely change mine the most because of my family and blood connections. There was no better way to put it. It was a match made in heaven. In every action, every custom, every detail – even in the way of cooking (I was there to cook at my friend Zaiyu Hasegawa's world-famous DEN) – I felt Japan in my bones and flesh. Each trip taught me more, even from something as simple as a cup of tea. And each time, I brought home something that made me a better chef and a better person.

Oteque is the sum of all these parts: a Brazilian restaurant deeply influenced by Japanese kaiseki ideology, striving to use local ingredients and to showcase the Mata Atlântica and its issues to the best of our ability, while remaining fair to my team, suppliers, and the environment.

I always say that a restaurant is a balance of three equal parts: it must be as pleasurable for my suppliers, staff and customers. If this formula bends too far to one side, Oteque won't be doing its job properly. As for this book, I hope the same balance is felt as you go through the witty writing of Andrea Petrini, the three voices – me, Rob and Andrea – and now you, the reader. May you have as much of a blast reading these pages as we had creating them. I hope you all enjoy the Oteque book. Here's to you!

18

# ACIDITY

Scallop, Leek, Tucupi

Pork Belly, Green Beans,
Pickled Shallots, Cabbage

Langoustine Tartare

Lamb's Leg, Caramelized
Brazil Nut Milk, Cabbage

Lamb Rump, Glazed Aubergine

Heart of Palm, Molasses
Vinaigrette

Grouper Confit, Carrot

Chocolate Sorbet, Pear

58

# TEXTURE

Slipper Lobster,
Corn, Saffron Sauce

Oyster, Pork Spine
Broth, Pork Skin

Octopus, Dried Tomato,
Brazil Nut

Cassava Cream, Shiitake,
Farofa de Mandioca

Grouper, Corn "Cuscuz",
Parsley

Coconut Sorbet, Acerola

Broccoli, Dried Yeast,
Honey Vinaigrette

Boudin Blanc, Mushroom Cream

Beetroots, Cashew
Cream, Cured Pork

Beef Tartare, Caramelized
Brazil Nut Milk, Shiitake

102

## BLOCKS

Tuna, Fish Mayonnaise, Caviar

Squid, Shimeji, Vegetable Cream

Shrimp, Pirão, Pimenta de Cheiro

Seabass, Fermented Tomato

Red Mullet, Parsley, Foie Gras

Mussels, Carrot

Grouper, Seaweed, Caviar

Duck, Apples, Jussara Cream

150

## LEADERSHIP

Yogurt Ice Cream, Apple

Wagyu, Shiitake Mushrooms

Beetroot Tartlet

Trout Roe Tartlet

Truffle Tartlet

Sand Perch, Endive, Vegetable Cream

Peach Sorbet

Oyster, Pimenta de Cheiro Vinaigrette

Oyster, Brazil Nut Milk, Caviar

Oyster, Green Apple

Oyster, Oyster Emulsion

Oyster, Heart of Palm

Porcini Mushrooms, Egg Yolk

Blackberry Sorbet, Beetroot Syrup

196

## CREATIVE PROCESS

Sweetcorn Ice Cream

Sea Urchin, Onion, Mussel Cream

Scallop, Fish Mayonnaise

Duck Heart, Beetroot Cream

Cashew Cream, Coconut Foam, Trout Roe

Brioche, Sardine, Foie Gras

Brazil Nut Ice Cream

Snapper, Kale, Heart of Palm, Pumpkin Seed

Açaí Sorbet, Rapadura Crumbs

01

# ACIDITY

It is said that great writers, the kind who leave their mark on the world and are remembered by future generations, were also avid readers before they became writers. So, do filmmakers – visionaries of the big screen such as Almodóvar, Coppola, Scorsese, Todd Haynes and Lars von Trier – ensconce themselves in dark theatres, film libraries, art and arthouse cinemas, and bury themselves in historical movies, retreating from the real world, in order to find their creative voice? Although these are rhetorical questions, in the case of Alberto Landgraf – the great Brazilian chef – the answer is no.

A leading chef on the culinary scene, not only in Latin America but worldwide, he has reached the relatively mature age of forty-something. In Brazil, he runs the restaurant Oteque in a very un-touristy neighbourhood of his adopted city, Rio de Janeiro, proving with remarkable singularity that there is always more than one way. That the tortuous path to a dream lies, more often than not, along a straight road. With the sharp perception of a truly atypical chef, he is oblivious to the fact that, in his spare time, he is also a great customer. "One thing has always puzzled me. Today, with these long and seemingly endless tasting menus, I often find myself feeling sated and tired after just three or four dishes. There's nothing worse than feeling like you're being held hostage at the table for hours, not wanting another mouthful, but you still have to keep eating. It's a kind of torture."

Alberto Landgraf has always remained faithful not to an esoteric search for the philosopher's stone, but to the fundamental principle at the heart of the contemporary cook that he is: the exact definition and judicious use of acidity. For him, it is not a gimmick. It is definitely not just a decorative finishing touch – adding a few drops of vinegar or lemon is not enough to superficially camouflage a dish – but rather a guiding principle that reflects his understanding and respect for taste. "It's true: acidity is like a compass for me, showing me true north, how and where to go. It's the main – how should I put it? – principle of how I run my kitchen. I have rules, reference points and concepts, principles around which I organise how I work at the stove. And, in a changing world, in which it seems there are no longer any common rules that act like a watershed between letting yourself go and simplification, and the latest fads, I care about principles. Incidentally, *Principles* was, for quite a while, the working title for this book."

**In the beginning, was there acidity?** Landgraf's path has been unique: an agile and analytical mind, his background in science should perhaps have led to a career in theoretical physics, but he dropped out before he was even halfway through. He ended up in a kitchen, accepting the risks that destiny brings. He is part of what we might call an "in between" generation. Too old to ride the Viking wave of Nordic cuisine, and too young to have been part of the legions trooping through the revolutionary upheavals of yesteryear's *conquistadores* in Catalonia's culinary labs: "One of the biggest regrets of my life is never having been to El Bulli." You can't win them all. And maybe it is for the best. Instead, in the early 2000s, Landgraf found himself in a very unusual middle position: at the top cooking stations of London's best kitchens, which were at the height of the Modern British movement, with the likes of Gordon Ramsay ("whose restaurant on Royal Hospital Road was in its golden years. What a privilege it was to see him toiling like a madman at the stove!"). And in 2003, he worked at Tom Aikens' first eponymous restaurant in Chelsea, shortly after it opened. "I might be part of the last generation of chefs to be classically trained, learning the basics of the trade: how to tame fire and to make perfect sauces. Those who have come afterwards, in line with these days of excessive prepping and mise en place, the challenge of cooking à la minute, and the sensuality of cooking, seem to me to have missed out on this. I learned so much at Tom Aikens. Back then, it was the most talked-about restaurant in London and certainly the most demanding. The working conditions were so intense that to say they were 'very intense' would be an understatement. Everything was governed by an overwhelming pressure and a quest for perfection. If I had to recognise a mentor, albeit a putative one, it would undoubtedly be him." He adds, with due respect that does little to hide his deep affection: "The experience at Aikens was exceptional. Particularly for someone like me who comes from a farming family that has always lived in contact with nature, far from city centres. My mother was Japanese and was very forgiving. My father, whose grandfather was German, was much stricter. He was a staunch believer in discipline. And I was certainly not disciplined. I went to a private Catholic school for years, excelling in almost every subject, but everything seemed easy to me, and I'd be lying if I said that I applied myself or studied hard. The nuns told me: you need rules, you need to be disciplined in life. Do some sport and take up volleyball. With a coach at your side and clear goals for both your body and mind, you'll be able to focus better on your studies, preparing you for the life that lies ahead. I started training, and I still do quite a bit of sport when I can. Working at Tom's was in its own way a kind of combat sport, like stepping into the ring. It was an initiation into the industry, but a tough one. He wasn't one of those chefs who explains things calmly and clearly, showing you what to do. Instead, you had to follow him into the thick of the action and prove you were up to it. You had to try to understand the hows and the whys of everything. If you could keep up with him, great; otherwise, you were out of your depth. I must say that in my twenties, my brain was like a sponge, absorbing and processing everything. I was fascinated by Tom, not only because his cooking was so complex that it verged on the perilous – you had to be on the alert all the time – but also because his dishes often had a liveliness and hint of acidity. He was obsessed with seasoning everything with salt, sugar and lemon, and with that as a starting point for an ingredient, we had to build mouth-watering flavours. A way of cooking, like mine is now, that when you taste it, is like a jolt to the brain."

**So, acidity.** A freshness that awakens the taste buds, stimulating them over and over again, demanding an "encore" as curiosity and greediness are roused; but so is the ability to analyse, to distinguish the various components of the dish in front of you with a total and always acute clarity of flavour. As one of the central elements of Alberto Landgraf's cuisine – if not at its core – this hint of acidity comes through in many forms. Not always in the most conventional ways. It is all part of a creative, contemporary approach with clear Brazilian roots, whose essence is always present, scattered but evenly spaced. Put into perspective. There's nothing "in your face": if it creates little immediate emotion, for Landgraf that is a ruse for avoiding anything that is picture perfect. "Obviously, I'm not rejecting my Brazilian identity, but I assert my freedom not to be defined solely by its best-known characteristics and products. I have little belief in, or affinity with, the claims of a cuisine that seems to me to be based only on a supposed endogenous identity that is essentially validated by ingredients found in anthropologically defined territories. Rio de Janeiro is not Amazonia, which is a world unto its own, still partly unexplored, with an ancestral culture all its own. Importing fish, herbs and unusual species by getting others to forage there makes little sense. It would even be contradictory for a restaurant like Oteque, which uses vegetables from artisanal farms near Rio, to do so. Fish and seafood make up a large part of our repertoire, and we have privileged access to fishers who have worked almost exclusively for us for years. Our menu generally consists of no more than eight courses, with only one meat dish to mark the transition to dessert; all the preceding courses are essentially seafood-based. Extraordinary ingredients, freshness of flavour is anathema to contrived culinary processes. Their brininess creates a dialogue with acidity, enhancing and even embodying that additional acidic freshness. This can, of course, be found in citrus fruit and different types of vinegar. But not only those."

Among Alberto Landgraf's favourite ingredients is honey, and it is always present. Not so much to add a subtle sugary undertone, but to extract from it a particular, unprecedented kind of acidity. But there is honey and honey: "Brazilian honey is very special – I'd say it's unique. Because of the local climate, which is extremely humid, it has a much higher water content than European honey, which is why it lends itself so well to the process of fermentation. You let time run its course and this allows a range of nuances to develop that even lean towards a subtle form of acidity. It's ideal for my style of cooking. After three years of fermentation, you begin to see the first changes. But if you give it two or three more years, that acidity – that's quite singular – becomes much more perceptible, and is something that only fermentation can bring about. I'll let you in on a secret – it's not actually legal to sell fermented honey in a commercial capacity in Brazil. That's why I ferment honey at home. It's such a precious commodity that I take good care of it within my four walls. I confess that I have a cupboard full of it at home, waiting for time to pass."

**Brazilian diners** – and an increasing number of international ones – jostle for one of the few coveted tables at Oteque, having quickly become familiar with Landgraf's dishes that are flavoursome but never arrogant, deceptively simple and always brimming with umami. It is not an obsession, but neither is it an end in and of itself. If anything, it is a way of anchoring that unstable element, which for this chef has become absolutely essential: ensuring a dish is balanced. Fermentation is one of the processes employed – one of many – but is never dominant. "It's not about going against the tide, nor is it to surprise or be annoying, and to tell the truth, I'll even admit to not being a great fan of fermenting. More often than not, I find it overpowering, exaggerated and forced, which risks everything tasting the same. We don't ferment grains, and we don't make miso all the time. Despite my Japanese roots and the umami that's evident in my dishes, and despite my love for that magnificent, strange, lunar country, which I adore and visit at least twice a year to see friends and to nourish myself culturally, cooking together at special events at their restaurants, I hardly ever – never say never – use traditional Japanese ingredients in my own restaurant, not even the most common, like soy sauce. Again, this is not to be a purist or to be interesting. But if what stands out the most is umami, used to stimulate the appetite with its savoury flavour, it doesn't make sense because you end up with the opposite effect, saturating the palate. And the same goes for fermentation. As I said, we're not crazy about it and only use fermented ingredients when there's no alternative, for particular results that can't

otherwise be achieved. Take tomato juice, for example. Made from a fruit with a lot of flavour. We ferment tomatoes to temper their extreme sweetness, which, in my opinion, can also make you get tired of them. We don't add anything; it's the natural fermentation process that reduces the 'sugariness' by producing a vibrant acidity."

**Nature and culture.** Hardly a prisoner of an irreconcilable duality, Alberto Landgraf's way of thinking boldly explores the entire vocabulary of a country that has a wealth of produce. He pays tribute to a peculiar form of seasonality, which more accurately should, if anything, be called "non-seasonality". What to do with the immense pantry of a country almost the size of Europe, covering 8.5 million square kilometres and filled with contrasts – climatic, geological, economic and social – ranging from the poor region of Belém in the far north with its humid tropical temperatures, to the lush green hills of Curitiba, often called Brazil's Switzerland? If sourcing as locally as possible is not just a voluntary act but an everyday practice that has been fought for and won, then the climatic specificity of Rio de Janeiro must be taken into account. Tourist brochures do not mislead when they boast about and advertise the high temperatures because Copacabana and all of Rio's other beaches are packed 365 days a year. "It sounds like a cliché, but it really is always summer in Rio. There are maybe two weeks or so in June when the temperature drops to around 22 degrees, which would be our winter! But then it's hot again. Temperatures are over thirty degrees throughout the rest of the year. Here, it's a joke to talk about seasonality. It's not like in Europe, where each season is characterised by produce that is in harmony with the changing climate and different terrains: tubers and roots in winter, and peas and asparagus announcing the arrival of spring. In Rio, tomatoes, peppers, aubergines and so on are found year-round, always on hand, you know ... they're always there. From one month to the next, the level of flavour doesn't change with the weather, it's usually pretty much the same. For me, there's nothing worse than being lazy and sticking to the same flavours. It's therefore necessary to diversify and try not to repeat the same ingredients in a menu, while also varying the way they are prepared and presented to bring out the best of each individual one. It's about pushing it to the max and interpreting it in the most expressive way," confesses this bespectacled chef, who would happily trade in his form-fitting black T-shirts and wear layers of warm flannel overshirts under a heavy jacket in the chilly cold of London many more times a year than he can.

For Landgraf, his time in England was his *bildungsroman*, when he came of age in the kitchens of the Old World that were his new university, discovering, with his now lifelong friends Isaac McHale of the Clove Club and James Lowe (formerly of Lyle's), the seasonal profusion found in the UK's farmers' markets. And with it, the importance of how cutting out the middle-men served to build relationships between cooks and producers, to create fraternities to which he was an eyewitness in those early days. In the megalopolis of Rio, Brazil's heritage really is something you come face to face with on a daily basis. A race against the normal flow of time. But it takes time to escape from the pressures of routine. To reflect, to think, to experiment. To remind oneself; and you do not have to be Einstein to realise how relative time always is. There is that of the long term, of the stream of consciousness, of creative introjection. And there is that of immediacy, of the natural mastery of one's vocabulary, handed down from father to son.

An iconic example would be Maison Troisgros in Roanne. Speaking about this legendary French restaurant, this Brazilian chef, who uses superlatives sparingly, has fond memories. "If I were forced to publicly reveal where I had the most satisfying dinner, in the truest sense of the word, out of all the three-star restaurants in the world, I would say Maison Troisgros without hesitation. The chefs there were the first in France, and indeed the world, to develop a keen awareness of acidity. Think of their great classic creations – salmon with a velvety sorrel sauce, a signature dish since the early 1970s – but also the way they studied vinegars and citrus juices that have always been a part of their dishes," says Landgraf, who continues, his eyes lighting up and his enthusiasm growing as he reminisces. "It was the first time I'd been there. A few years before COVID, I agreed to accompany Thomas Troisgros to Roanne to visit his grandfather and cousins. Pierre, the patriarch, was still there, and his son Michel had not yet handed over the reins of the kitchen to César, who is almost my age. And the restaurant had not yet moved to its new location in Ouches. More than the fantastic dinner itself, I remember that the following morning, Thomas, César and I went with Michel to the market in Roanne. In the summer, there was a wide variety of produce and Michel would get excited and brag: 'I do the shopping, and based on what I find I'll decide what to make for you tonight.' He bought some magnificent plums that were chosen deliberately not quite ripe, and pickled them in vinegar that day to enhance their sweetness and give them that hint of acidity that they, like me, are so fond of. I was amazed at the simplicity of that approach, and by how they were spoilt for choice with so much produce available. It all seemed too easy for someone like me, who was used to battling every day with the obstacles that I faced to get supplies."

Long gone are those early years. Since February 2018, Oteque has shone from Rio to well beyond the nation's borders. But apart from specialists and historians of contemporary cuisine, few know that fate smiled on this young man – who didn't have much money at the time – from the moment he embarked on his career. The calm that comes from anonymity was not something he experienced, and much less the advantages that come with the uncertainties of starting out. As soon as he returned to Brazil – not to Rio, but São Paulo, the country's economic and cultural capital – and before opening Oteque, he opened Epice, his first culinary atelier, which was met with dazzling success from both the public and critics. Epice, a small place, seating just thirty or so, became an immediate hit for both lunch and dinner and was even harder to get into after Brazilian journalist Alexandra Forbes ("I challenge you to find a better value-for-money lunch menu than the one offered at Epice in all of Brazil for €20.50."), whose instincts are legendary, gave it a glowing review:

"The future of Brazil's new cuisine has a name: Alberto Landgraf." For once, Michelin did not just stand by and watch, and the star that came shortly afterwards consolidated the chef's renown, also attracting attention from abroad. Those were the years of Brazil's great economic boom, and this was reflected in a culinary effervescence that began to bring local talents, such as Helena Rizzo, Alex Atala and Rodrigo Oliveira, into the spotlight. Epice was like a bombshell: such erudite cooking, imbued with a well-understood European heritage that was strange to Brazilian palates, had never been seen before: it publicly squared the circle, redefining the country's identity through the prism of fruitful past experiences. Success has never turned its back on Alberto Landgraf since then. When he decided to leave São Paulo to be with his future (ex-) wife, he found that many of his clients followed him.

"Even today, many of Epice's first fans come here three or four times a year, asking if they can enjoy some of the dishes from São Paulo's golden years again. Except for very rarely, I always refuse. It's because I have to contend with current signature dishes, which would become new classics if I didn't change them at least every week. The move to Rio was not an insignificant one: here, there is the sea, and the fishers – saltwater as well as freshwater – work together closely. I've earned the trust of independent producers, of obscure indigenous communities. Fifteen years ago, the problem was complicated and totally the opposite, and I confess that, on returning home, I had no idea what Brazilian cuisine really was, because I didn't know my homeland that well. Exploring, discovering, tasting and getting an idea of the way in which Brazil is composed of myriad ethnicities, identities, cultures and social strata took years of travelling."

The words of a half-German and half-Japanese Brazilian with deep Italian roots. The French would call it a "creuset de cultures", and when he talks about indigenous ingredients and age-old techniques, he always does so with a mixture of constant curiosity and sincere respect. How could it be otherwise when you know that the local way of cooking is anything but an open book, punctuated by seemingly impossible ingredients in a repertoire of foodstuffs that have now been welcomed into the world of fine dining. Take *tucupi*, for example. A liquid derived from manioc (the dried solids are used to make a traditional white flour, similar to tapioca) that must first be boiled. It has a slightly lactic, vaguely acidulous flavour, common to so many familiar and popular recipes and dishes. "For me it's probably the wildest Brazilian ingredient there is," explains Landgraf. He loves it, but, like all his fellow cooks, he rightly does not even try to make it. "It's a matter of respect, but also of knowledge. Manioc contains – like cinnamon, did you know that? – a small amount of cyanide that, however small, you must know how to eliminate. Leaving it a few days to ferment. When the Portuguese landed here to colonise us more than 550 years ago, the native peoples were familiar with the laws of fermentation, and they have been used in their villages, every day, perhaps for thousands of years. It's part of their cultural heritage."

With the past nourishing the present, popular culture is trying to resist the steamroller of being adopted by the West. There is an iron logic to Alberto Landgraf's cultural universe. And, lingering in the shadows, is a spirituality not entirely removed from an unexpected sense of self-derision. We do not know if Landgraf signed up to lie on a therapist's couch between sittings, but it would certainly benefit many of his celebrity colleagues and other chefs who would benefit from a little introspective hindsight on their life and therefore on their work (in restaurants and elsewhere). But, in these times of extreme self-care, perhaps he already has a tailor-made diagnosis: "The job I do requires a lot of concentration, you really must apply yourself. I have financial and moral obligations with employees, official relations with the government and institutions. Jumping from one thing to another, between the flattery on social media and customers, a cook often ends up taking himself too seriously. Perhaps my penchant for self-mockery comes less from a form of modesty – yes, and back to my fixation again – than from a natural affinity with acidity. That again, but understood here not only from a gustatory point of view but also from a cultural one. Maybe it was the years of being weaned from Brazilian humour when I was in the UK, but I'm now extremely receptive to British humour. The British are naturally eccentric, sometimes a bit stiff, but at least they hardly ever take themselves seriously. They have their own particular way of being beneficially ironic. An irreverence that could be described as 'sour', acidic in fact. Think Ricky Gervais or Monty Python, but also the edgy, acerbic and often funny style of the best British journalism. Like the food writing of Giles Coren and the late A. A. Gill. As a maniacal perfectionist, I'm rarely happy about myself and about my work, which could always be perfected. But at least I don't think that I'm goodness knows who. But my grumpy old-man nature lets me make fun of myself. I confess to being a big fan of TV presenter Jeremy Clarkson, in particular of his series *Grumpy Old Men*. You'd be hard pressed to find someone more acidic, no, even more corrosive than him."

In short, Alberto Landgraf knows how to choose good company. More Walter Matthau than Jack Lemmon (referring to the former, "he was the one grumbling and making fun of practically everybody"), he embodies the figure of the young Wise Old Man. He can't be tricked. It is his chicness: ironic and acidulous that starts with himself. A lucid sourness, perhaps a tad self-conscious. But all the wittier for us all.

Scallop, leek, tucupi
→ p. 48

Grouper confit and carrot
→ p. 54

Langoustine tartare
→ p. 50

Pork belly, green beans, pickled shallots and cabbage

→ p. 49

**Lamb's leg, caramelized Brazil nut milk, cabbage**
→ p. 51

Lamb rump, glazed aubergine
→ p. 52

Heart of palm, molasses vinaigrette

→ p. 53

Chocolate sorbet, pear
→ p. 55

# SCALLOP, LEEK, TUCUPI → p. 31

**For the scallops**
- 300g Vegetable Base (page 145)
- 6 scallops

**For the leeks**
- 2 leeks
- 60g olive oil
- salt, to taste
- 6 teaspoons toasted buckwheat
- lemon juice, to taste
- 3g picked and finely chopped parsley

**For the tucupi**
- 300g tucupi
- 200g butter
- 200g Fish Base (page 145)
- salt

**Scallops**
Reduce the vegetable base in a saucepan to a glaze. Shuck the scallops and clean away all the guts, then rinse under cold running water to remove any remaining grit or sand. Skewer the scallops and leave them to reach room temperature, then grill one side over hot embers for about 1 minute, until they start to caramelize. Glaze the grilled side with the reduced vegetable base and return to the grill for about 30 seconds until completely caramelized.

**Leeks**
Preheat a steam oven (100% steam) to 90°C (194°F). Remove the green parts and the roots of the leeks and remove the outer layers. Put the leeks in a vacuum bag with the olive oil and a pinch of salt, seal and cook in the steam oven for 50 minutes. Remove the leeks from the bag and sear in a hot frying pan over a high heat with a drizzle of olive oil. Remove and, once cooled to room temperature, cut them into 5mm cubes.

**Tucupi**
Reduce the tucupi to 200g in a saucepan over a low heat, add the butter and the fish base, then remove from the heat and emulsify with a stick blender. Season with salt.

**Finish**
Mix the leeks with the toasted buckwheat and season with lemon juice and salt. Add the parsley. Heat the tucupi and froth it with a stick blender.

**Serve**
Arrange 1 tablespoon of leek and one scallop (grilled side up) on a plate and spoon the tucupi foam around the scallop.

—

**Carbon footprint**
tucupi 30.61%; scallops 28.18%; butter 16.8%; vegetable base 7.96%; olive oil 6.65%; fish base 4.03%; leeks 2.58%; salt 2.57%; buckwheat 1.52%; lemon juice 0.07%; parsley 0.03%
**Total emissions per serving**
0.7kg $CO_2e$

# PORK BELLY, GREEN BEANS, PICKLED SHALLOTS, CABBAGE → p. 37

- 100g green beans, blanched and finely chopped
- 9 Pickled Shallots (page 145), cut into wedges
- 180g Pork Neck Base (page 144), reduced to a thin glaze
- sorrel leaves, to garnish

**For the pork belly**
- 100g fine sea salt
- 1kg water
- 2kg skinless pork belly
- 5 thyme sprigs
- 100g olive oil
- 1 garlic clove

**For the cabbage**
- drizzle of olive oil
- 1 small green cabbage, cut into 6 wedges (keep the core intact)
- salt, to taste

**Pork belly**
Make a brine with the salt and water in a 10cm-deep 1/3 gastro and immerse the pork belly in the brine. Store in the refrigerator for 7 hours. Drain away the brine and put the belly, thyme, olive oil and garlic in a vacuum bag. Seal under full vacuum and cook in a water bath at 75°C (167°F) for 7 hours. Refrigerate, then divide into twelve 6 x 3cm pieces.

**Cabbage**
Heat a drizzle of oil in a frying pan over a high heat, then sear the cabbage wedges on one side until completely caramelized. Season with salt.

**Finish**
Sear the belly portions in a hot frying pan on one side, without any fat or oil, until they caramelize, then put them straight on serving plates (2 pieces per person).

**Serve**
Add one seared cabbage wedge to each plate, then add 2 tablespoons of chopped green beans (in 3 piles) and 5 pickled shallot wedges. Finish with 2 tablespoons per serving of pork neck glaze and garnish with the sorrel leaves.

—

**Carbon footprint**
pork belly 66.35%; salt 14.47%; pork neck base 8.49%; cabbage 4.98%; olive oil 3.73%; green beans 0.92%; pickled shallots 0.71%; water 0.13%; thyme 0.13%; garlic 0.06%; sorrel leaves 0.03%
**Total emissions per serving**
1.39kg $CO_2e$

# LANGOUSTINE TARTARE → p. 35

**For the langoustine tartare**
- 300g cleaned langoustine tails (50g per person)
- salt, to taste
- lemon zest, to taste
- 10g Shio Kombu (page 147), finely chopped, to serve
- burnet saxifrage leaves, to serve

**For the pickled green apple**
- 1 green apple, peeled and cut into 2mm cubes
- 100g Simple Syrup (page 146)
- 100g white vinegar

**Langoustine tartare**
Cut the langoustine tails into small pieces, being careful not to mince it – the texture of the flesh must be preserved.

**Pickled green apple**
Combine the cubed apple with the simple syrup and vinegar in a vacuum bag and seal under full vacuum.

**Finish**
Mix the chopped langoustine in a bowl with the pickled green apple and season to taste with the salt and lemon zest.

**Serve**
Place the seasoned langoustine in a round single layer on a flat plate. Finish each dish with a pinch of shio kombu and burnet saxifrage leaves covering the entire surface of the tartare.

—

**Carbon footprint**
langoustine 64.68%; simple syrup 14.93%; shio kombu 7.64%; white vinegar 6.85%; green apple 4.15%; salt 1.49%; burnet saxifrage leaves 0.16%; lemon zest 0.1%
**Total emissions per serving**
0.38kg $CO_2e$

# LAMB'S LEG, CARAMELIZED BRAZIL NUT MILK, CABBAGE → p. 40

- 6 tablespoons Caramelized Brazil Nut Milk (page 144)
- 6 tablespoons Beef Shin Base (page 144), reduced to a thin glaze
- olive oil, for drizzling, to serve
- wild watercress leaves, to serve

**For the lamb's leg**
- 1.5kg lamb's leg
- salt, to taste
- 100g olive oil
- Beef Shin Base (page 144), reduced to a thin glaze, for brushing

**For the cabbage**
- drizzle of olive oil
- 1 small purple cabbage, cut into 6 wedges (keep the core intact)
- salt, to taste

**Lamb's leg**
Preheat a steam oven (100% steam) to 90°C (194°F). Place the lamb's leg with the salt and olive oil in a vacuum bag and seal under full vacuum. Cook in the steam oven for 7 hours 30 minutes. Remove the lamb from the steam oven and let it cool at room temperature. Preheat a dry oven to 200°C (392°F). Once the lamb has reached room temperature, remove it carefully from the bag and brush it all over with the reduced beef base. Roast it in the dry oven for 7 minutes. Brush with the reduced beef base again and return to the dry oven for another 7 minutes at the same temperature. Remove from the oven and let it rest for 5 minutes, then debone and slice into 6 equal portions before serving.

**Cabbage**
Heat the drizzle of oil in a frying pan over a high heat, then sear the cabbage wedges on one side until completely caramelized. Season with salt.

**Finish and serve**
Place the lamb on one side of the plate and place a seared cabbage wedge next to it. Place 1 tablespoon of the Brazil nut milk near the meat and finish with 1 tablespoon of the reduced beef base, a drizzle of olive oil and some wild watercress leaves.

—

**Carbon footprint**
lamb's leg 84.71%; beef shin base 12.28%; olive oil 1.38%; caramelized Brazil nut milk 0.92%; cabbage 0.41% salt 0.29%; wild watercress 0.01%
**Total emissions per serving**
9.62kg $CO_2e$

# LAMB RUMP, GLAZED AUBERGINE → p. 41

- 100g Beef Shin Base (page 144), reduced to a thin glaze
- 5g lamb fat (see method)
- 50g toasted buckwheat
- pea shoots, to garnish

**For the lamb rump**

- 600g lamb rump
- 50g butter
- bunch of thyme sprigs
- drizzle of olive oil
- salt, to taste

**For the glazed aubergines**

- 3 medium aubergines
- olive oil, for brushing
- 150g white vinegar
- 150g honey
- 6g salt

**Lamb rump**

Trim the lamb to give it a more uniform shape, then put it in a vacuum bag with the butter, thyme sprigs and some salt. Seal under full vacuum and cook in a water bath at 60°C (139.6°F) for 1 hour 10 minutes. In the meantime, put the lamb trimmings in a pan and place over a low heat, to render the fat. Reserve the fat for later. Rest the lamb at room temperature for 15 minutes, then immerse it (still in the bag) in iced water and leave it for 15 minutes. Preheat the oven to 200°C (392°F). Remove the lamb from the iced water and from the bag, then sear it all over (turning it) in a frying pan over a high heat with the drizzle of olive oil before transferring it to the oven (still in the frying pan) and roasting for 3 minutes.

**Glazed aubergines**

Preheat the oven to 180°C (356°F). Halve the aubergines lengthways and mark each half in a crosshatch pattern to a depth of about 2mm. Brush the aubergines with olive oil, season with the salt and roast in the oven on a roasting tray for 20 minutes. Increase the oven temperature to 200°C (392°F). Combine the vinegar and honey in a bowl, brush the aubergines with the mixture and return to the oven for 5 minutes. After 5 minutes, brush the aubergines again with the mixture and return to the oven for 5 more minutes. Repeat this process until the aubergines are completely caramelized.

**Finish**

Cut the lamb into twelve 1.5cm-thick slices. Cut each aubergine half into 2 rectangles, the same size as the slices of lamb. Heat the beef shin base in a saucepan over a low heat and add 5g of the lamb fat extracted from the trims. Stir vigorously.

**Serve**

Place two slices of lamb and two slices of aubergine on the plate. Sprinkle a pinch of toasted buckwheat on top of the glazed aubergine slices and finish with the beef sauce on and around the lamb. Garnish with pea shoots.

—

**Carbon footprint**

lamb rump 75.55%; beef shin base 17.02%; aubergines 3.11%; olive oil 1.26%; white vinegar 0.85%; honey 0.74%; butter 0.63%; salt 0.56%; toasted buckwheat 0.19%; thyme 0.13%; pea shoots 0.02%

**Total emissions per serving**

4.62kg $CO_2e$

# HEART OF PALM, MOLASSES VINAIGRETTE → p. 43

**For the heart of palm**
- 450g fresh hearts of palm
- 50g olive oil, plus extra for drizzling
- 4.5g salt

**For the molasses vinaigrette**
- 300g molasses vinegar
- 100g olive oil

**To serve**
- green wood sorrel leaves
- nasturtium leaves
- nasturtium flowers
- mizuna leaves or Japanese mustard greens
- Peruvian black mint leaves
- 20g untoasted hazelnuts, chopped (peel away as much of the outer skin as possible)

**Heart of palm**
Preheat a steam oven (100% steam) to 100°C (212°F). Put the hearts of palm, olive oil and salt in a vacuum bag, seal under full vacuum and cook in the steam oven for 45 minutes. Remove the hearts of palm from the bag and cut each into 3 equal pieces. Sear the heart of palm pieces in a very hot frying pan with a drizzle of olive oil.

**Molasses vinaigrette**
Reduce the molasses vinegar in a saucepan over a low heat until it reaches a syrupy consistency, being careful not to burn it. Let it cool and set aside. In a bowl, mix one part of this syrup with one part olive oil.

**Serve**
Place 4 pieces of the heart of palm on the centre of the plate and add 1 tablespoon of the molasses vinaigrette on top. Finish with all the green leaves and flowers and the hazelnuts.

—

**Carbon footprint**
heart of palm 64.77%; olive oil 18.46%; molasses vinegar 13.78%; hazelnuts 1.55%; salt 1.3%; green wood sorrel leaves 0.03%; nasturtium flowers 0.03%; nasturtium leaves 0.03%; Peruvian black mint leaves 0.03%; mizuna leaves 0.03%
**Total emissions per serving**
0.65kg $CO_2e$

# GROUPER CONFIT, CARROT → p. 34

**For the grouper confit**

- 1 grouper, cleaned, gutted and filleted (70g fillet per serving)
- generous amount of olive oil, the best you can get
- salt, to cure

**For the roasted carrots**

- 3 carrots (various colours if you can), peeled
- 150g butter
- 15g thyme sprigs
- salt, to taste

**For the carrot sauce**

- 300g carrot juice, made fresh with a juice extractor
- 30g molasses vinegar
- squeeze of lemon juice
- pinch of salt
- pinch of Shio Kombu Powder (page 147)
- a few drops of Kombu Oil (page 146)
- a few chives, finely chopped

**Grouper confit**

Coat the fish fillets generously with salt and transfer to the refrigerator for 8 hours. Wash the cured fish under cold running water and, with the skin intact, wrap it tightly with cling film. Slice it into roughly 70g portions – ideally you get a perfect round, as this helps all the fish-flesh cells align – then put the cling-film-wrapped slices in a 10cm-deep 1/3 gastro. Cover the sliced fillets with the olive oil (they should be fully immersed) and cook in a steam oven (100% steam) at a low heat (about 42°C/107.6°F) for 15 minutes. Remove from the gastro and let it rest at room temperature to finish cooking and develop a shimmer and delicate appearance.

**Roasted carrots**

Preheat the oven to 150°C (302°F). Put the whole carrots in a 2.5cm-deep 1/2 gastro with the butter, salt and thyme and roast in the oven for 1 hour 30 minutes. Turn the carrots every 30 minutes to caramelize on all sides. Remove from the oven and cut the carrots into 2cm pieces.

**Carrot sauce**

Heat the carrot juice and the molasses vinegar in a saucepan until gently simmering, then season to taste with the lemon juice, salt, shio kombu powder, kombu oil and chives.

**Finish and serve**

Place the grouper confit in the middle of the plate and arrange pieces of roasted carrot alongside. Finish with 1 tablespoon of the carrot sauce around the fish and over the carrots.

—

**Carbon footprint**

salt 80.62%; grouper 10.47% butter 3.72%; olive oil 1.97%; carrots 1.01%; carrot juice 0.87%; molasses vinegar 0.54%; shio kombu 0.37%; kombu oil 0.27%; lemon juice 0.08%; thyme 0.07%; chives 0.01%

**Total emissions per serving**

2.35kg $CO_2e$

# CHOCOLATE SORBET, PEAR → p. 45

**For the chocolate sorbet**
- 110g black Dutch-processed cocoa powder
- 74g cocoa butter
- 500g water
- 5.2g salt
- 1.4g guar gum
- 0.5g xanthan gum
- 140g sugar

**For the pear crisp**
- 1 pear
- 300g Simple Syrup (page 146)

**For the rapadura crumbs**
- 100g rapadura
- 100g ground almonds
- 100g black Dutch-processed cocoa powder

**For the pear compote**
- 500g Simple Syrup (page 146)
- 6g ground turmeric
- 4 pears

**For the pimenta de cheiro compote**
- 150g sugar
- 300g water
- 4 pimenta de cheiro

**Chocolate sorbet**
Blend the cocoa powder and cocoa butter in a Thermomix until smooth and set aside. Put the measured water, salt, guar gum, xanthan gum and sugar in a saucepan and heat over a low heat for 3 minutes until the sugar has dissolved, stirring constantly. Pour the warm mixture into the Thermomix containing the cocoa powder and cocoa butter and blend at low speed, gradually increasing the setting until it reaches high speed. Blend for 5 minutes. Place in a Pacojet beaker and leave in the refrigerator for 24 hours, then freeze at -18°C (0°F). Spin twice before serving.

**Pear crisp**
Slice the unpeeled pear thinly using a mandoline and combine the slices with the simple syrup in a vacuum bag. Seal under full vacuum, then remove, spread all the slices out on a Silpat and dehydrate in a dehydrator at 60°C (140°F) for 24 hours.

**Rapadura crumbs**
Preheat the oven to 100°C (212°F). Finely grate the rapadura, mix it with the ground almonds and cocoa powder and roast in a shallow gastropan for 1 hour. Let the mixture cool to room temperature, then blend in the Thermomix at high speed until crumbs form.

**Pear compote**
Bring the simple syrup to the boil in a saucepan with the turmeric, and while it cools down to room temperature, peel the pears, slice them lengthways into four equal pieces and remove the seeds. Combine the pears and the turmeric simple syrup in a vacuum bag, seal under full vacuum and cook in a water bath at 45°C (113°F) for 30 minutes. Cool in an ice bath and reserve.

**Pimenta de cheiro compote**
Dissolve the sugar in the measured water in a saucepan over a low heat. Slice the pimenta de cheiro lengthways, remove the seeds and add the pimenta to the syrup. Cook over a low heat in the syrup for 2–3 minutes, or until tender but firm to the bite. Drain away the syrup and slice the pimenta into small cubes (as small as you can).

**Serve**
Place 1 teaspoon of rapadura crumbs in the middle of the plate and shape a quenelle of chocolate sorbet on top. Place a dehydrated pear slice beside the sorbet and on the other side, some pear compote. Finally, add ½ teaspoon of pimenta de cheiro compote on top of the sorbet.

—

**Carbon footprint**
simple syrup 28.93%; sugar 18.73%; black Dutch-processed cocoa powder 28.39%; cocoa butter 10%; rapadura 5.65%; pears 3.69%; ground almonds 3.16%; salt 0.63%; pimenta de cheiro 0.37%; ground turmeric 0.25%; water 0.09%; guar gum 0.08%; xanthan gum 0.03%
**Total emissions per serving**
1.56kg $CO_2e$

02

# TEXTURE

Imagine one evening at dinner. Even at night, Rio de Janeiro is still wrapped in a warm quilt. The taxi slows down just a few metres from an unassuming apartment block. Outside, there are few signs, no obvious indication of a restaurant waiting for us inside. Set in a bustling working-class neighbourhood still buzzing with energy in the early evening, Oteque eventually reveals itself to the visitor, provided they look closely at the metal plaque on the wall next to the entrance. It's hard to be more inconspicuous. Discretion is an understatement for this destination restaurant. Which makes the contrast between the outside and the inside like a little big bang. Once inside, the space is loft-like with a cosy, almost suspended ambiance, in stark contrast to the large area. Punctuated by round tables, this space, which dates from 1934, was a warehouse back in the day. The walls, all made of rectangular bricks framed by pale wooden panels rising to form a triangular attic shape, still evoke the building's past industrial heritage. The kitchen, at the far end of the room, draws the eye into a calm, open scene devoid of grand statements. It is bordered by the chef's table for just a handful of customers, who can closely observe the action: a front row seat to all the activity that goes on around the stoves. Elegance is celebrated through informality and the absence of luxurious frills, focusing instead on the lines and volumes that are essential. This feeling is not immediate but becomes clear gradually. Perhaps it is the absence of ostentatious elements and the intimate, relaxed atmosphere that makes one sense something definitely unusual in the air. A fine-dining restaurant on a human scale, so human that it must have been tailor-made. Alberto Landgraf, as we know, is not one to leave much to chance. And that not only goes for what is on the plate. He is a man of principle who works with ingredients and all the elements at his disposal to shape their textures. Textures. No matter what kind they are.

"Right from the beginning, I knew that Oteque had to be different from most other restaurants. It had to encapsulate me down to the smallest detail. Including those hardly visible to the naked eye. After studying the space at length and where the tables should go, I spent a small fortune on a suitable lighting system to ensure it was bright yet not aggressive, as if it were a balmy caress. It's a question not just of intensity, but also of consistency. Something almost palpable," says Landgraf. This implicitly suggests a sensation that we could translate as follows: light as a variation in the density of the air. He used the same approach for the room's acoustics: "I wanted sound to be an integral part of the experience, and to be clearer, I use this term – experience – which I normally abhor. At Oteque, music is one of its building blocks. Always present but never too loud or intrusive. Nor is it a banal backdrop serving as an accompaniment to fill the space; it is crisp, has a life of its own, winds its way through the room like a layer of sound yet respects the table conversations of the diners. It has a texture, a thickness – an ever-changing consistency all of its own."

Texture – one of Alberto Landgraf's main guidelines. Not quite an obsession, but rather the multifaceted strategy of a chef wanting to escape the routine and boredom associated with it, and who always prefers the liveliness of surprise. Excitement in each mouthful, in the act of chewing. He plays, right from the design phase of a project, with variations of mouthfeel for each dish. We could call it the incessant repetition of differentiation. This involves modulating what each individual ingredient offers and how it is treated. If the proposition at Oteque is presented as a medium-length menu, it is because Landgraf does not believe in taking diners hostage. And even less, he confirms with a caustic smile, in producing Stockholm syndrome. "Restaurants that kidnap customers always lose them in the end. You can have too much of a good thing. Four hours seated at a table, enduring plate after plate, is a concept that represents an era that is now over. Whether we're reading a book, watching a film or having an evening meal, we all have a more or less limited attention span. You must be careful not to exceed two and a half hours, which, in my opinion, is already a very long time for a well-structured dinner. I and the team eliminated everything superfluous, of course. Snacks, a relic of false generosity and cheap opulence, serve no purpose except to distract the palate's attention, right from the start. It's better to get straight to the point by starting with the first course on the menu. There's excitement – and then concentration – for the dinner that will follow all the way to the meal's zenith."

Clothes do not make the man, yet it is always the first impression that counts. The menu at Oteque, printed and laid out on the table for diners to see, seems to reveal everything but actually discloses only the essentials. Or little more. Just the titles of the dishes, three or four ingredients used per course, rarely more, punctuated by vertical slashes that bring them into line. A preview reminder of what will soon follow. It steps away from the tacit rules and usual mental constructions that typically define the rigid framework of a restaurant with such ambitious standards. At Oteque, which prides itself on serving the freshest seafood and the finest "marine game" sourced directly from its network of fishers, traditional expectations are subverted, established hierarchies overturned. It is not just the dichotomy, so prevalent elsewhere, between sought-after cuts of fish and meat and other, far less prized natural ingredients, but also the dialogue, the physical confrontation between disparate elements. On this late summer evening, the pungent seaweed vinaigrette is the perfect accompaniment to the raw dusky grouper, with its firm, almost sashimi-like texture, with the pine nuts and caviar providing a contrasting sweetness like a little explosion. With the second course, the flavours become more daring. The oyster's supreme milkiness extends the meaty side of things via its own version of surf-and-turf, with a concentrated pork stock made from ribs and gelatinous pork rind – a joyful mix of contrasting textures. But where does the oyster end and the pork rind, which is as mellifluous as can be, begin? And wouldn't the pork ventresca with potatoes and Amazonian walnut emulsion have been placed almost at the end of the menu in any other restaurant in the world? There is obviously a very disruptive logic behind this.

It is no coincidence that those who know him well have affectionately nicknamed Alberto Landgraf "the Thinking Chef". His head tells him what interests him and his gut tells him what he likes. When he declares, "I detest monocultural dishes," you might think that he isn't keen on most risottos, for example, because more often than not, each forkful tends to be the same. "When I say that monocultural dishes don't appeal to me – and I'm using this term not really knowing whether it's correct or if it really exists, in which case I'll take the liberty of inventing a concept – it's to express a sense of boredom that I feel when a dish has only one, predominant, texture. In my opinion, you need at least two complementary elements that can interact with each other. The real issue is not the surprise effect or technical wizardry, but the natural balance of the dish itself. If you're working with a soft texture, which will caress the palate, you need to contrast it with something crunchy. Conversely, if you start with a crunchy element, it's a good idea to add an extra dimension by using a silkier element to create a textural contrast. This will amplify its singularity. The two must relate as equals."

What he doesn't state explicitly is how this basic concept evolved over time. Perhaps it is rooted in the preferences he has had since childhood, such as the crunch of dried fruit or crunchy Amazonian nuts, or it may come from later discoveries. When in search of his Japanese heritage, he indulged in the most renowned sushi in Tokyo, and discovered the unparalleled timeless elegance of Kyoto-style kaiseki cuisine. He'd also steal away to hole-in-the-wall shops, unseen and unrecognised, that were within walking distance, giving in to the temptation of bags of pork jerky. Everyone has their guilty pleasure, their addiction, and this is his: very fine, crispy yet slightly chewy dried pork flakes – not exactly junk food but more a tempting treat for those who love to chew.

Let's indulge ourselves in a flashback. And let's imagine the young Landgraf as an apprentice in Gordon Ramsay's kitchens during his time in England, where perfection went hand in hand with a subtle sweetness and the purest textures. "Each dish was impeccable, a flawless work of art, to borrow the words used in ads of the day. I still think back to all those lobster ravioli with their bisque or with tomato chutney that I meticulously prepared for years. They were magnificent, more than perfect, but in my opinion, what was glaringly missing was a lack of asperity to counter the consistency." Things were another kettle of fish in Tom Aikens' kitchen. In the early 2000s, he seemed to be chasing a chimera trying to square the circle, synthesising perfectionism while seeking to combine the classicism he learnt from working hunched over and side by side with Joël Robuchon with the experimental techniques emerging from Catalonia. "Tom never aimed to be like Ferran Adrià; his restaurant didn't aspire to become the new El Bulli, but in those years he was certainly the chef who, from a technical standpoint, pushed the envelope more than anyone else on the scene in the UK. I remember it as if it were yesterday: his dishes were a tour de force, built around a single ingredient – carrots, for example – treated in myriad ways: braised, puréed, grilled, oven-dried, powdered and emulsified. His almost obsessive, and sometimes excessive, approach reassured my natural interest and curiosity for textures.

Alberto Landgraf never seeks inspiration from traditional sources or from techniques validated by being commonly used. Rather, his ideas stem from the fruitful observation of everything around him, whether it be nature, reverence for an ingredient or the free flow of thought, and not being wedged in by the usual class divisions. What if lower class culture was truly an integral part of this Brazilian chef's conceptual horizon? He implicitly admits this himself when he says that his long pondering on pork jerky was the creative spark for a dish that customers immediately appreciated for its unmistakable savoury freshness. However, it would be difficult to speak of immediacy honestly. "I started with the assumption that I was not the only person in the world who unashamedly enjoyed eating pork jerky. Wanting to deliver something reminiscent of it, but in a more refined way that would not clash with the idea of fine dining, I started thinking. Trying. Using beef, for example, it was first braised, then dried before being cut into a very thin slice and placed in the middle of the plate. Flavoursome, almost crunchy, it had an 'other' texture. It was enlivened with pickled baby onions and a hint of honey drizzled all around. While the cause-and-effect relationship was not obvious and could not be compared to the Japanese snack, the inspiration was definitely transferred." Landgraf also enjoys extracting a particular meatiness from beetroots, which are cooked gently sous vide for hours until they have acquired a very chewy consistency  and an earthy umami that is like a briny nod to the sea. "Its texture is similar to that of dried beef, which goes very well with cashew cream. The base is slightly sweet and is made simply with water and a little oil, providing an interesting, velvety contrast to the meatiness of the beetroot. When I speak of textures, I mean the term in its broadest sense, encompassing many textures, not just crunchiness."

Alberto Landgraf speaks the truth and nothing but the truth. For him, this admiration for contrasts can rarely be described with the word "rupture". And it is even more rarely achieved via an unoriginal cause-and-effect relationship. Instead of cutting-edge technology and a plethora of preliminary preparations, he much prefers manual craftsmanship, treating ingredients with a delicate approach. Cooking times can be quick and intense or, conversely, slow and gentle over smouldering embers, making use of the residual heat. The use of fire always reflects the natural characteristics of the desired end product. And that includes raw cooking. Like his scallops. Blended three times and then frozen, the process is repeated two more times before the flesh is ready ("without a single drop of oil or salt, I swear") and transferred to a piping bag. The results are small rings, like rubber bands, which are then flattened with a rolling pin before being rolled up and sprinkled with a few grains of salt and quickly done in the oven: "Until they are translucent and have a wonderful silky texture, halfway between the sweetness of seafood and the concentrated flavour of umami."

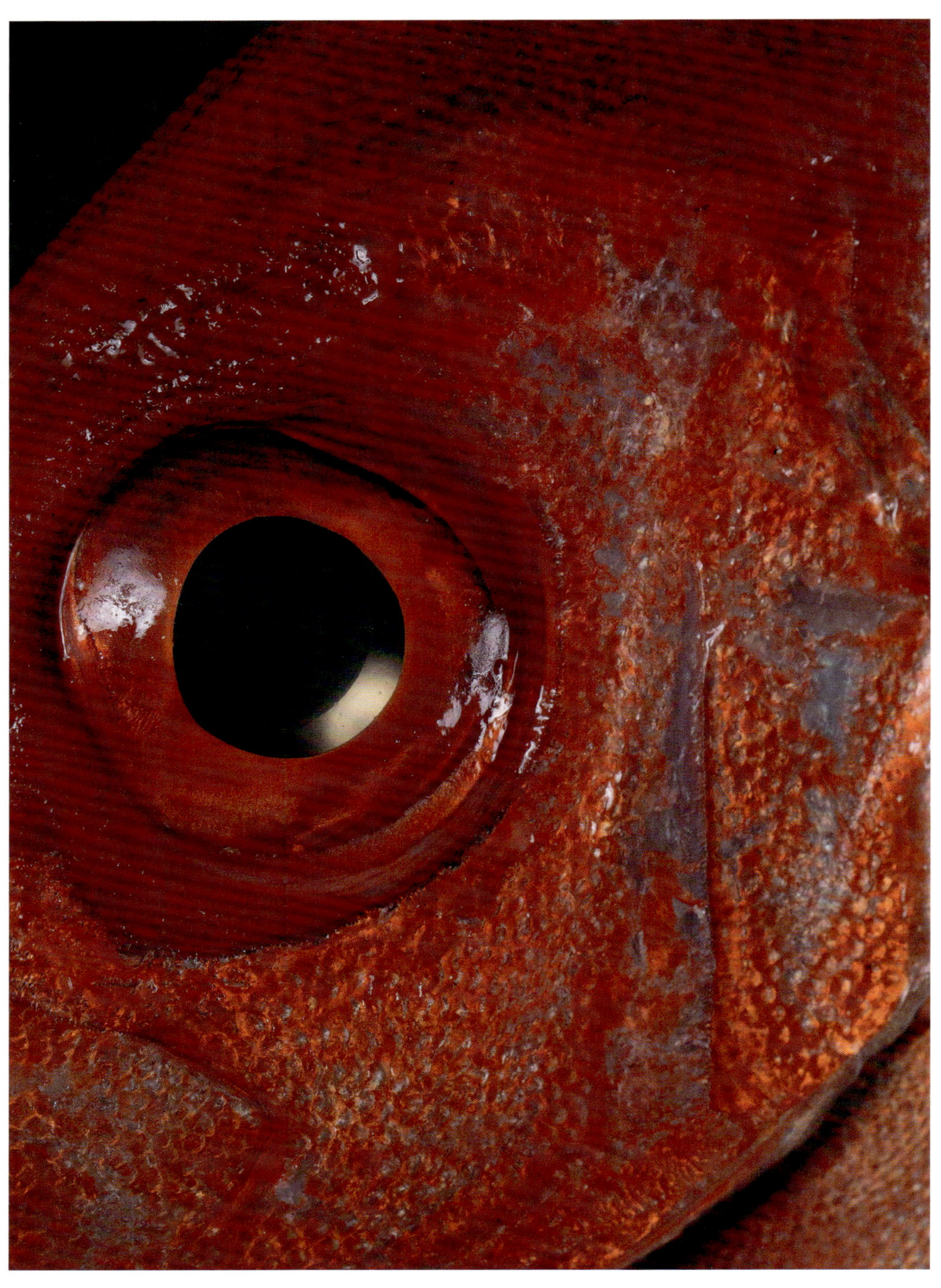

He tames the fire, takes its pulse, and then practically steps aside, letting the intrinsic essence of the ingredient express itself. Landgraf is not the only one with a soft spot for squid. Ductile, they readily lend themselves to being prepared in many ways, but choosing one way, supposedly a priori one as the best, makes little sense for a chef who knows that the art of cutting is often the actual genesis of the dish. "I learnt this cutting technique, an incision almost as if drawn by the squid itself, first hand in Japan. The tentacles are cooked separately using a relatively aggressive process to make them crispy, while the central body of the squid is cooked more gently to ensure it remains tender and to guarantee good chewability. In this case, the interplay of textures is dictated by the ingredient itself; no divine intervention is required, just precise cooking. The different textures on the plate interact with each other, providing a varied experience with every bite. The same technique lends itself to other ingredients. White mushrooms, for example, which, when served with the various parts cooked separately and differently, can result in both soft and crispy textures. And even shiitakes, dehydrated overnight on the barbecue as the embers die. The next morning, when we get to the kitchen, they're crispy on the outside and slightly chewy on the inside. Perfect with a dash of vinegar and a drizzle of ginger oil."

He'd make his life easier if he weren't so intransigent about quality and not such a stickler about naturalness: "Whether it's cooked for a long time or not, an ingredient must always express its identity. Our approach starts by limiting the use of fats, and we use as little as possible. Our stocks are all vegetable-based and we use tiny amounts of butter and only as needed." But he is an athlete of the unexpected, of contingencies. A trump card turned into a virtue out of necessity. Of course, he could unashamedly adopt the famous maxim of Alain Ducasse – a highly accomplished chef but culturally very different – gleaned from his many years of experience, which advocates observing everything that comes and grows from the earth: "Cook well what is good in the garden, and use only natural, seasonal ingredients that can be found as locally as possible." What's the point in complaining about bad luck when, for obvious reasons of hygiene – given the high temperatures in Brazil – the mullet delivered to the restaurant has already been gutted? Alberto explains: "It's a pity, but mullet liver is banned here; you just can't use it. It really is impossible to find. By law, before being sold or delivered, all fish must be gutted immediately after being caught. Obviously, this means that I lose some of the characteristic bitterness of the mullet's liver, but at the restaurant I replace it with chicken liver, which is less strong. However, I can still achieve interesting velvety textures by binding it with a parsley emulsion – the same one I use for my duck heart dish. Unfortunately, this isn't the only example of an ingredient that's impossible to find. Unlike in Europe, the culture of offal and popular, hearty dishes using what the Italians call *il quinto quarto*, doesn't exist here for the reasons I just mentioned. Of the ingredients that can be used in so many different ways and offer so many different textures, offal is obviously at the top of my list of things I'd like to my customers to be able to try. I love it, but for the moment it's out of the question."

It is one of the paradoxes of Brazil, and this is reflected at Oteque, a destination restaurant that specialises in creative, signature cuisine. The Amazonian region has a wealth of indigenous ingredients and produce, and there is a constant search for a sustainable supply: this then goes hand in hand with the need for them to be translated with a view to creating fine dining experiences with international appeal. Because beyond the regulars and other Brazilian customers, most of those visiting Oteque come from far and wide, from every Latin American country, from the US and from Europe. Like many others, Landgraf could change the menu to a year-round "best of" selection. However, the drive to create goes hand in hand with mindful reasoning. "Traditionally, we consume a lot of beef, and it is also exported all over the world. I like meat and I'll happily eat it; I don't condemn animal protein, but as a cook, I find that there's nothing more boring to cook. At Oteque, veal will never be the main course; it will never be the predictable highlight of the menu. If anything, it will become part of other recipes but very discreetly. I select only the best animals, paying extreme attention to traceability and the conditions in which they are raised. I buy only carcasses that allow me to use every part of the animal. The goal is to escape routine, to always innovate and never repeat the same things or preparations. Our regulars, many of whom are from Rio, as well as those who come from elsewhere, sometimes several times a year – couples, with friends, for business dinners or for celebrations – would notice immediately."

And what else can be done when, in an age that raves so much, rightly or wrongly, about databases and storytelling, Alberto Landgraf has a devoted audience that has followed him right from the start and would not miss a season? His most loyal customer "is a widower in his sixties. He comes alone every Wednesday evening and has never missed a week since Oteque opened in 2018. He doesn't even look at the menu or ask for anything special; he just trusts us. In an age where people are always trying to take your picture and post it on Instagram, this gentleman is an exception: a man of few words, he only talks with the sommelier, and doesn't even ask for me to go over and chat. Customers like him may be an exception, but being able to satisfy someone for years and years is extremely rewarding." The success of this cutting-edge restaurant, which, to paraphrase Paganini, never repeats itself, is also measured by its diverse clientele of all ages and cultures, and is forever changing – like the interplay of textures on the plate. Bring in the young people, but, come on, make way for older people too. They were not born yesterday and you can't trick them. And for them, perhaps more than others, because they've been around the block a few times, routines just don't cut it.

Slipper lobster, corn, saffron sauce
→ p. 90

Oyster, pork spine broth, pork skin
→ p. 91

**Octopus, dried tomato, Brazil nut**

→ p. 92

Cassava cream, shiitake, farofa de mandioca
→ p. 93

**Grouper, corn "cuscuz", parsley**
→ p. 94

Broccoli, dried yeast, honey vinaigrette

→ p. 96

Boudin blanc, mushroom cream
→ p. 97

**Beetroots, cashew cream, cured pork**
→ p. 98

Beef tartare, caramelized Brazil nut milk, shiitake
→ p. 99

Coconut sorbet, acerola
→ p. 95

# SLIPPER LOBSTER, CORN, SAFFRON SAUCE → p. 69

**For the slipper lobster tails**
- 1kg water
- 100g fine sea salt, plus extra to taste
- 3 slipper lobster tails, peeled and cleaned
- Shrimp Base (page 145), reduced to a thin glaze, for brushing

**For the baby corn**
- 6 baby corn, cleaned
- 100g butter
- salt, to taste

**For the saffron sauce**
- 500g double cream
- 0.2g saffron threads
- squeeze of lemon juice
- salt, to taste

**Slipper lobster tails**
Dissolve the fine salt in the water in a 10cm-deep 1/3 gastro to make a brine and immerse the slipper lobster tails in the brine for 3 minutes. Drain and slice the fillets lengthways, then grill on one side over hot embers for 40 seconds. Brush the ungrilled side with the shrimp glaze and return to the embers with the glazed side down for 40 seconds.

**Baby corn**
Preheat the oven to 120°C (248°F). Put the corn in a 10cm-deep 1/3 gastro with the butter and some salt and confit in the oven for 30 minutes or until tender. Slice thinly lengthways.

**Saffron sauce**
Combine the cream and saffron in a saucepan and cook for 40 minutes over a low heat. Strain through a chinois and season with the lemon juice and salt.

**Serve**
Place the saffron sauce in the middle of the plate and assemble a grilled slipper lobster tail half on one side and on the other side, the sliced baby corn.

—

**Carbon footprint**
lobster 37.04%; salt 27.69%; double cream 22.76%; butter 8.09%; baby corn 3.65%; shrimp base 0.42%; water 0.25%; lemon juice 0.05%; saffron 0.05%
**Total emissions per serving**
0.72kg $CO_2e$

# OYSTER, PORK SPINE BROTH, PORK SKIN → p. 71

- 6 shelled oysters (large, if possible)

**For the pork skin**
- 200g coarse sea salt
- 20g thyme sprigs
- 3 garlic cloves, peeled
- 800g pork skin

**To serve**
- 300g Pork Spine Broth (page 144), heated
- Porcini Oil (page 146), for drizzling

**Pork skin**
Mix the coarse salt, thyme sprigs and garlic in a bowl. Use a sharp knife to remove as much fat from the underside of the pork skin as possible, then turn it over and use a blowtorch to burn off any hairs. Cover the pork skin with the salt mixture and leave it to cure in a sealed container for 2 hours in the refrigerator. Rinse the cured skin and cut it into 20cm squares. Place in a vacuum bag, seal under full vacuum and cook in a water bath at 85°C (185°F) for 12 hours. Remove it from the bag, and once it has reached room temperature, scrape the remaining fat from the underside. Cut the skin into smaller 10cm squares, stack in piles of 6 squares, wrap tightly in cling film and gently arrange inside a vacuum bag. Seal under full volume and freeze. Once frozen, unwrap each pile and slice into thin strips using a meat slicer.

**Oyster**
Steam the shelled oysters at 90°C (194°F) for 4 minutes, then transfer straight to the serving bowl.

**Serve**
In the bowl that holds the cooked oyster, stack 8g of sliced pork skin on top of the oyster and pour enough hot pork spine broth to cover the oyster (the skin will get hot with the temperature of the sauce). Drizzle with some porcini oil to serve.

—

**Carbon footprint**
pork skin 65.61%; salt 20.05%; pork spine broth 9.44%; oysters 2.69%; porcini oil 1.97%; thyme 0.12%; garlic 0.12%
**Total emissions per serving**
1.88kg $CO_2e$

# OCTOPUS, DRIED TOMATO, BRAZIL NUT → p. 73

**For the fermented tomato oil**

- 50g Fermented Tomato Powder (page 147)
- 200g rapeseed oil

**For the octopus**

- 1 whole octopus (2–2.5kg)
- olive oil, for drizzling
- bunch of thyme
- 5g salt
- 10g Fermented Tomato Base (page 147), reduced to a thin glaze, for brushing

**For the dried tomatoes**

- 30 sweet grape tomatoes
- olive oil, for drizzling
- sugar, to taste
- salt, to taste

**To serve**

- 6 tablespoons Caramelized Brazil Nuts (page 144)
- mizuna leaves or Japanese mustard greens

**Fermented tomato oil**
Blend the tomato powder and oil in a Thermomix at high speed for 1 minute, then decant through a chinois overnight.

**Octopus**
Poach the whole octopus in a large saucepan of boiling water for about 1 minute. Cool it on ice, then cut off 6 tentacles. Put the tentacles in a vacuum bag with a drizzle of olive oil, the thyme and salt, seal under full vacuum, and cook in a water bath at 82.2°C (179.7°F) for 2 hours 45 minutes. Prepare an ice bath, transfer the bag of tentacles to the ice bath, then, once cool, remove the tentacles from the bag and sear them in a hot frying pan with a drizzle of olive oil until caramelized. Brush them with the fermented tomato glaze.

**Dried tomatoes**
Score an 'x' in the bottom of each tomato and blanch them in boiling water, then peel away the skin. Spread them out on a baking tray and season each tomato with a drizzle of olive oil and a pinch of salt and sugar. Dehydrate in the oven at 85°C (185°F) for about 1 hour 30 minutes.

**Serve**
Arrange an octopus tentacle on the plate glazed side up. Add 1 tablespoon of the caramelized Brazil nuts next to the tentacle, then assemble the dried tomatoes beside the tentacle in a way that follows the shape of the tentacle. Cover the dried tomatoes with drops of fermented tomato oil and finish with mizuna leaves on the tomatoes.

—

**Carbon footprint**
rapeseed oil 34.33%; caramelized Brazil nuts 25.78%; octopus tentacles 14.52%; sweet grape tomatoes 10.59%; olive oil 6.95%; salt 4.08%; fermented tomato powder 1.74%; thyme 0.84%; sugar 0.73%; fermented tomato base 0.35%; mizuna leaves 0.09%
**Total emissions per serving**
0.42kg $CO_2e$

# CASSAVA CREAM, SHIITAKE, FAROFA DE MANDIOCA → p. 75

**For the cassava cream**

- 500g cassava
- 200g butter
- 150g milk
- salt, to taste

**For the dried cassava**

- 100g cassava
- 100g water

**For the farofa de mandioca**

- 50g butter
- 150g cassava flour
- 1.5g salt
- 2g chives, finely chopped

**To serve**

- 6 teaspoons Shiitake Confit (page 146)
- fresh black truffles, for slicing

**Cassava cream**

Cut the cassava into 3mm-thick slices. Place the slices side by side (not stacked or overlapping) inside a vacuum bag and seal under full vacuum. Cook in a water bath at 71°C (159.8°F) for 1 hour. Remove from the bag and rinse the cassava under cold running water to remove the starch. Put the cassava in a saucepan, cover with water and cook over a medium heat until soft (this can take 1–3 hours). Strain and blend in a Thermomix at 60°C (140°F) at high speed with the butter, milk, and salt to taste, until smooth.

**Dried cassava**

Blend the cassava and water in a Thermomix on high speed until smooth. Transfer to a saucepan and cook over a low heat for 8–10 minutes until it reaches a sticky consistency, stirring every 5 minutes. Spread it out on a Silpat in a thin layer and bake in the oven at 120°C (248°F) for 1 hour 30 minutes until completely firm and dry. Break into large pieces and reserve in a sealed container.

**Farofa de mandioca**

Melt the butter in a frying pan over a medium heat, add the cassava flour and salt and toast, stirring, for 2 minutes. Turn off the heat and finish with the finely chopped chives.

**Finish and serve**

Heat the cassava cream and arrange 2 tablespoons to the side of the plate with 1 teaspoon of shiitake confit on top. Lay 1 teaspoon of farofa de mandioca over the confit and finish with a sprinkle of the dried cassava and 5g of sliced truffle.

—

**Carbon footprint**

milk 28.8%; butter 27.14%; cassava 14.63%; truffles 12.86%; butter 6.79%; shiitake confit 3.58%; cassava flour 3.26%; salt 2.85%; chives 0.05%; water 0.04%

**Total emissions per serving**

0.43kg $CO_2e$

# GROUPER, CORN "CUSCUZ", PARSLEY → p. 76

**For the grouper**

- 100g fine sea salt, plus extra to taste
- 1kg water
- 420g cleaned, gutted and filleted grouper, cut into 6 portions (70g each)
- 300g Fish Base (page 145)
- 300g Vegetable Base (page 145)
- drizzle of olive oil, for brushing

**For the corn "cuscuz"**

- 300g corn flocão
- 10g sweet cassava starch (tapioca starch)
- butter, to taste
- salt, to taste

**To serve**

- 3g chives, finely chopped
- 60g Parsley Emulsion (page 147)
- 5g purple and green wood sorrel leaves

**Grouper**

Dissolve the fine salt in the water in a 10cm-deep 1/3 gastro to make a brine, immerse the portioned fillets and leave to brine for 8 minutes. Combine the fish and vegetable bases in a saucepan and simmer until reduced to a thin glaze. Drain the brine away and dry the fillets with a paper towel, then brush them with olive oil and season with a sprinkle of salt. Cook over hot embers for 2 minutes, or until cooked, turning them frequently so they don't burn. Once cooked, brush the glaze on one side of the grouper and return to the embers briefly to caramelize.

**Corn "cuscuz"**

Mix the corn flocão and starch in a bowl and hydrate, little by little, with water until you can form a ball that holds its shape and no longer absorbs water. Transfer the mixture to an airtight container and rest in the refrigerator for 30 minutes. Add more cold water, little by little, until the mixture is softer and spreadable. Preheat a steam oven (100% steam) to 100°C (212°F). Spread the mixture out in a perforated gastronorm and cook in the steam oven for 40 minutes, then scrape the cooked "cuscuz" with a spoon until it forms fine crumbs. Season with butter and salt.

**Serve**

Place a 6cm ring on the plate and fill it with corn "cuscuz". Top the corn with the chopped chives. Arrange 1 tablespoon of parsley emulsion beside it and finish with the grouper fillet, grilled side up. Garnish the dish with wood sorrel leaves in the middle of the plate.

—

**Carbon footprint**

grouper 36.16%; salt 28.5%; corn flocão 15.27%; vegetable base 8.12%; fish base 6.16%; olive oil 2.55%; parsley emulsion 1.99%; butter 0.69%; butter 0.68%; water 0.26%; sweet cassava starch 0.13%; purple wood sorrel 0.09%; chives 0.07%

**Total emissions per serving**

0.68kg $CO_2e$

# COCONUT SORBET, ACEROLA → p. 87

- elderflowers, to garnish

**For the caramelized coconut**
- 270g fresh coconut meat (peel away the outer skin as much as possible), cut into 1cm cubes
- 120g water
- 360g sugar

**For the fresh coconut milk**
- 3kg fresh coconut meat (peel away the outer skin as much as possible), cut into pieces
- 3kg room-temperature water

**For the coconut sorbet**
- 1kg coconut milk
- 80g sugar
- 100g liquid glucose
- 5g isomalt powder
- 10g dextrose powder
- 500g fresh peeled coconut meat
- 60g lemon juice

**For the coconut parfait**
- 1kg coconut milk
- 100g sugar
- 7 bloomed gold gelatine leaves
- coconut sorbet (above)

**For the dehydrated coconut**
- 1kg coconut milk
- 200g coconut milk powder
- 100g sugar
- 8g iota carrageenan

**For the acerola consommé**
- 1kg washed and destemmed acerola
- juice of 1 lemon, or to taste

**Caramelized coconut**
Mix all the ingredients in a frying pan over a medium heat and cook until the sugar dissolves and the cubes of coconut start to caramelize. Stir constantly and continue cooking until the sugar crystallizes and becomes dry. Remove from the heat.

**Fresh coconut milk**
Put the coconut pieces and the water in a Thermomix and blend at medium-high speed for about 2 minutes until smooth. Strain through muslin and reserve.

**Coconut sorbet**
Put the coconut milk, sugar and glucose in a saucepan, place over a low heat, add the powders and cook for about 7 minutes, stirring continuously, until the mixture thickens. Let it cool in the refrigerator. Once cold, blend the coconut base with fresh coconut meat and lemon juice in a Thermomix at high speed for about 4 minutes, then strain through a tamis (drum sieve). Place in a Pacojet beaker and freeze at -18°C (0°F). Spin once before serving.

**Coconut parfait**
Put the coconut milk and sugar in a saucepan and dissolve the sugar over a low heat, then remove from the heat and add the bloomed gelatine leaves. Stir until the gelatine has dissolved. Transfer to a 10cm-deep 1/3 gastro, cover and chill until firm. Put in a siphon with two N2O (nitrous oxide) charges. Wrap a 6cm diameter (5cm deep) ring with cling film, sealing the bottom, then fill the ring with the mixture right up to the top. Smooth the surface with a spatula and freeze at -18°C (0°F). Using a warm ice cream scoop, create a cavity in the frozen parfait and fill it with coconut sorbet. Return to the freezer.

**Dehydrated coconut**
Put all the ingredients in a Thermomix and blend at high speed until it reaches 70°C (158°F). Put the mixture in a stand mixer fitted with the whisk attachment and whisk until it is cool and has reached a firm consistency. Spread the mixture out in a thin layer on a Silpat and dehydrate in a dehydrator at 60°C (140°F) for 12 hours. Break into 5cm square pieces and reserve in a sealed container.

**Acerola consommé**
Mash the acerolas with a masher – or use your hands – and strain through a muslin. Decant the liquid overnight in the refrigerator through a muslin-lined chinois to clarify it. Season with lemon juice.

**Finish and serve**
Place the bowl in the freezer to get cold and remove the parfait from the freezer to warm it up a little (remove the ring before serving). Put the parfait in the middle of the plate and place the caramelized coconut on top. Place the dehydrated coconut pieces around the parfait and pour the acerola consommé around the parfait. Garnish with elderflowers.

—

**Carbon footprint**
sugar 39.45%; fresh coconut meat 27.16%; acerola 13.22%; coconut milk powder 10.01%; liquid glucose 3.97%; gelatine leaves 3.87%; lemon juice 0.69%; dextrose powder 0.55%; iota carrageenan 0.44%; isomalt powder 0.28%; water 0.04%; elderflowers 0.02%
**Total emissions per serving**
1.64kg $CO_2$e

# BROCCOLI, DRIED YEAST, HONEY VINAIGRETTE → p. 81

**For the broccoli**
- 24–30 stems of broccoli rabe, cleaned and trimmed
- olive oil, for drizzling
- salt, to taste

**For the honey vinaigrette**
- 70g lemon juice
- 140g honey
- 200g rapeseed oil
- 2g xanthan gum

**To serve**
- Dried Yeast (page 146), for sprinkling
- broccoli flowers, to garnish

**Broccoli**
Preheat the oven to 200°C (392°F). Season the broccoli with a little salt, drizzle with olive oil, spread out on a roasting tray and roast in the oven for 7 minutes, or until crunchy.

**Honey vinaigrette**
Blend the lemon juice and honey in a Thermomix at medium speed, then gradually add the rapeseed oil to thicken. Add the xanthan at the end, while still blending, to stabilize the mixture.

**Serve**
Place 1 tablespoon of the honey vinaigrette in the middle of the plate, add 4–5 roasted broccoli stems over the honey, and sprinkle some dried yeast on top. Garnish with yellow broccoli flowers.

—

**Carbon footprint**
rapeseed oil 46.9%; olive oil 19%; broccoli 17.28%; honey 10.56%; lemon juice 2.91%; salt 2.48%; xanthan gum 0.6%; dried yeast 0.23%; broccoli flowers 0.04%
**Total emissions per serving**
0.3kg $CO_2e$

# BOUDIN BLANC, MUSHROOM CREAM → p. 83

- 2g purple wood sorrel leaves, to serve

**For the boudin blanc**
- 150g Chicken Wings Base (page 145)
- 6 dried shiitake mushrooms
- 300g boneless chicken breast, cut into small cubes
- 300g double cream
- 5g chives, finely chopped
- salt and freshly ground black pepper

**For the mushroom cream**
- drizzle of olive oil
- 1 shallot, finely chopped
- 1 leek, trimmed, washed and finely chopped
- 200g fresh shiitake mushrooms, cut into small cubes
- 100g fresh button mushrooms, cut into small cubes
- 150g white wine
- 1kg double cream
- 15g dried porcini mushrooms
- 15g dried shiitake mushrooms
- thyme sprigs, to taste
- squeeze of lemon juice
- salt, to taste

**For the heart of palm**
- 50g fresh heart of palm, cut into 1cm cubes
- 15g olive oil, plus extra for searing
- 5g salt, to taste

**Boudin blanc**
Bring the chicken wings base to the boil in a saucepan, remove from the heat, add the dried shiitake mushrooms, cover with a lid to retain the heat and leave for 30 minutes to hydrate. Slice the rehydrated, drained shiitake into small cubes (you can use the chicken wings base for another dish). Put the cubed chicken breast in the freezer for 15 minutes, then put it in the Thermomix and blend for 2 minutes at high speed. Add the double cream and mix again at low speed to incorporate. Pour the mixture into a bowl, add the cubed shiitake and chives and season with salt and pepper. Divide the mixture into three portions: working one portion at a time, place into a 30cm square sheet of ovenproof cling film, fold the film over to cover the filling and, using the film either side of the mixture, roll firmly on the bench into a log. Once it is about 7cm long, spin it by holding both ends, then tie to secure. Repeat with the remaining mixture to form three sausages. Twist each roll into sections to form smaller sausages, packing the sausage mixture tightly to avoid air pockets. Preheat a steam oven (100% steam) to 85°C (185°F). Cook the rolls in the steam oven for 25 minutes. Prepare an ice bath, place the steamed sausages in the ice bath in their cling film wrapping until cool, then cut the cling film between the sections and remove the rolls from the film.

**Mushroom cream**
Heat the oil in a saucepan over a high heat, add the chopped onion, leek and fresh mushrooms and cook for 4 minutes, until caramelized, then add the white wine and reduce until the mixture is almost dry. Add the cream, dried mushrooms and some thyme sprigs and cook, covered, over a low heat for 45 minutes. Pour into a Thermomix and blend at high speed until smooth, then strain through a chinois and season the cream with lemon juice and salt.

**Heart of palm**
Combine the cubed heart of palm with the olive oil and the salt in a vacuum bag, seal under full vacuum and cook in a water bath at 100°C (212°F) for 45 minutes. Remove from the water bath and the vacuum bag, then sear the cubed pieces of heart of palm in a frying pan with a drizzle of olive oil over a high heat.

**Finish**
Heat a drizzle of olive oil in a frying pan over a high heat and sear the boudin blanc on all sides.

**Serve**
Place 1 tablespoon of the fried heart of palm on the base of the plate and cover with the mushroom cream. Place the purple wood sorrel leaves on top of the mushroom cream and finish with one seared boudin blanc in the middle.

—

**Carbon footprint**
double cream 38.17%; chicken breast 22.73%; dried shiitake mushrooms 12.78%; white wine 6.93%; chicken wings base 4.94%; heart of palm 4.08%; olive oil 2.99%; dried porcini mushrooms 2.4%; leek 1.55%; fresh shiitake mushrooms 1.44%; salt 0.74%; button mushrooms 0.71%; black pepper 0.21%; shallots 0.19%; thyme 0.16%; chives 0.09%; purple wood sorrel 0.02%
**Total emissions per serving**
1.14kg $CO_2e$

# BEETROOTS, CASHEW CREAM, CURED PORK → p. 84

**For the beetroot cubes**
- 10 small beetroots
- olive oil, for brushing
- salt

**For the sliced beetroot**
- 1 large beetroot

**To serve**
- 150g Raw Cashew Nut Cream (page 144) (25g per person)
- Dried Yeast (page 146), for sprinkling
- 18 Cured Pork Belly slices (page 145), or other cured meat
- purple Egyptian star cluster flowers, to garnish

**Beetroot cubes**
Preheat the oven to 150°C (302°F). Brush all the beetroots with olive oil and season with salt. Place on a roasting tray and bake in the oven for 2 hours, then peel and cut each beetroot into four equal pieces.

**Sliced beetroot**
Preheat the oven to 110°C (230°F). Wrap the large beetroot in foil and cook in the oven for 1 hour. Let it cool in the refrigerator, then peel gently and, using a mandoline, cut into thin rounds about 6cm in diameter, making sure each slice is uniform.

**Serve**
Spoon the raw cashew nut cream on the plate and sprinkle 3g of dried yeast over it. Assemble 4 beetroot pieces on top, lay 3 slices of cured belly pork and finish with sliced beetroot rounds. Garnish with purple star cluster flowers.

—

**Carbon footprint**
cured pork belly 49.69%; raw cashew nut cream 33.26%; beetroot 8.23%; olive oil 6.52%; salt 2.12%; dried yeast 0.11%; purple Egyptian star cluster flowers 0.07%
**Total emissions per serving**
0.53kg $CO_2e$

# BEEF TARTARE, CARAMELIZED BRAZIL NUT MILK, SHIITAKE → p. 85

**For the wagyu tartare**

- 300g wagyu shoulder fillet (50g per person)
- 70g Shiitake Confit (page 146)
- 5g chives, finely chopped
- 70g Pickled Shallots (page 145), cut into small cubes
- 3g salt
- 2g black pepper
- 5g olive oil

**To serve**

- Caramelized Brazil Nut Milk (page 144)
- 6 pinches of Dried Yeast (page 146)
- 6 pinches of Mushroom Powder (page 146)
- fresh black truffle, for grating

**Wagyu tartare**

Cut the wagyu in small and uniform pieces, being careful not to mince it – the texture of the flesh must be preserved. Mix the beef in a bowl with the shiitake confit, chives and pickled shallots and season to taste with the salt, black pepper and olive oil.

**Serve**

Arrange the wagyu tartare in the centre of a plate in a round, single layer. Using a squeezy bottle, place 8 dots of caramelized Brazil nut milk on top of the beef (not too much), sprinkle gently with some dried yeast and mushroom powder, then, using a microplane, shave black truffle over the top until the beef is covered.

—

**Carbon footprint**

wagyu 96.88%; truffle 1%; shiitake confit 0.65%; caramelized Brazil nut milk 0.64%; shallot pickles 0.28%; mushroom powder 0.25%; olive oil 0.1%; salt 0.1%; black pepper 0.03%; chives 0.01%; dried yeast 0.01%

**Total emissions per serving**

5.54kg $CO_2e$

03

# BLOCKS

It is now the time to lay the cards on the table. To play the trump card. And to state, without fear of contradiction, that it would be difficult to find a more singular cook than Alberto Landgraf. As you leaf through this book, you will already have had an inkling of that. And those of you who frequent Oteque regularly are well aware of this. His relentless culinary approach is to categorise, to classify. Little corresponds to the intrinsic characteristics of Brazilian cuisine, which is focused essentially on ingredients, following the footprints of indigenous cultures, and on the myth of origins. If one asks around what the main idea is, what the source of inspiration is, even what the emotions imbued in their dishes are, many chefs – I'd venture to say most of them – will give an answer from a tired repertoire. The archaeology of the know-how of indigenous early cultures. The traditions of popular communities. Memories of family dishes. Or, trust in what is progressive and innovative: laboratory-like experimentation of raw materials using cutting-edge technology.
In *The Savage Mind* (1962), Claude Lévi-Strauss speaks of foraging, in other words, the pantheism of nature pressured by the dialectic of culture. Landgraf is no philosopher, no theatrical storyteller. Quite the opposite, if anything. Although he has studied applied physics, he will not evoke, as other experts do, the central idea of inertia from which his taste structures branch. But, in his own words, he will illustrate one of his main axes – and I quote: "the backbone" – of his cuisine. In a word: Blocks.

But what does that imply? What does it mean to create in the kitchen using "building blocks"? Well, it all starts with empirical observation, corroborated by his own personal experience. Let's go back to the days when he was sweating his guts out over the stove at the most important restaurants in the UK. *O tempora, o mores*... Oh, the times! Oh, the customs! Back then, the best restaurants hummed along à la carte – traditional recipes with different additions according to the season. The endless tasting menu was not yet on the horizon. Yet there were already, for those with the sharpest hearing, the astonished voices of some who had found – like St Paul on the road to Damascus – their vocation on the trail of a brilliant, obscure Catalan sorcerer. "Those were the years of the El Bulli explosion. Not only was there just one menu, the same for everyone, with space-like and otherworldly things, but the restaurant closed for five months of the year. Ferran Adrià wasn't taking a winter break, he was working flat out in his laboratory kitchens, assisted by a small group of collaborators. Together, they created a menu of twenty, thirty or even forty courses of dishes, snacks and morsels, which would be presented to diners when he reopened again in March until the end of October. So, in a nutshell, the idea of a collection would emerge, much like designers who create garments a year before they are available in boutiques. Despite my amazement, in a moment of clear-headedness, I wondered: When the season is over, what happens to all those recipes? Because I sensed that they would leave the scene, disappearing once and for all. I could already sense the looming pressure to constantly create. With technology becoming dominant, the expectation to always push the envelope would later influence the cooking congresses that were popular at the time, where chefs would appear on stage – like schoolchildren showing off their homework – to present their latest culinary creations. Always trying to be in the vanguard, never sitting still with their arms folded."

It was sort of, to put it in today's sensibility, the discovery of the unsustainability of such an approach; of that forging ahead, with the obligation of always having to explore new fertile frontiers. In hindsight, we know that rush to constantly create suffocated more than one chef. But Alberto Landgraf was still only halfway to his evolution. He had not yet worked out his "Blocks" strategy. He still lacked real-life experience. Let it never be said that he sinned out of impetuosity, out of impulsiveness. With the launch of his first restaurant, Epice in São Paulo, he went against the flow. Instead of going from theory to practice, he put what he had already learned during his years of training into practice. Studying its application in vitro. But despite the immediate, resounding success, this new kid in town felt that something wasn't right. "I'd just returned from England, used to the routine of calling suppliers by phone to place orders, getting everything that we wanted and was available. In Brazil, the situation was very different; the supply system was much bumpier, and there were many unpredictable variables. In the early days of Epice, we had a lot of dishes on the menu – far too many. To avoid running out of ingredients, I sometimes found myself having to freeze fish, which I did very reluctantly, as it made absolutely no sense to me. The blocks idea came about little by little. If it started from a basic need for more prudent management, it also led to a different creative approach," enthusiastically explains this Brazilian chef who then really did take the necessary time to reflect. When the time came to put a tiger in the tank, he closed Epice and went on training trips to northern Europe and Japan. This included an intensive stint at Noma – a leading restaurant in the field of organic experimentation – in Copenhagen, as well as several visits to the heart of everyday life in Japan, where the pursuit of minimalist perfection is evident in everything from three-star restaurants to the diligent cleaning of railway stations. In order to prepare for the much-anticipated opening of Oteque, which he describes as "starting a new professional chapter in a city like Rio that seemed like virgin territory to me, and where I decided to follow my then-wife, who was running two vegetarian restaurants there," he gave himself two years of in-depth self-reflection. This approach, which could be defined as mental sustainability, involved examining daily organisational problems and rationalising waste, while also addressing the age-old drive of creation. "From Epice to Oteque, times had changed. Firstly, because Epice started out as an à la carte bistro with a 'seasonal cuisine' formula pushed progressively to the highest level. In Rio, I knew I would be forced to rationalise that energy and offer a tasting menu. But as it was, the menu was too wasteful, too disorganised and no longer suited what I had in mind, yet I felt that the format of a tasting menu brought with it too many contradictions. How do you strike a balance between the short life expectancy of a menu presented to diners for just a few weeks, destined to disappear forever, and the pressure of not repeating yourself and adapting to situations and the hazards of everyday life and the market, while offering new culinary experiences? I didn't want to become a prisoner – like so many of my friends and colleagues – of organised changes at specific dates, or of a kind of scorched-earth rush to create a new collection from scratch every season. Anyway, this would not even have been possible in Rio, since the seasons change little or not at all here, and we have the same climatic conditions all year round. This deprives us of the huge shift in seasonal produce, fruit and vegetables that follow each other in accordance with the cycles of nature. I was looking for a system to resolve these contradictory demands. Then one day, quite by chance, my attention was drawn to a documentary on Lego that I saw on Vimeo."

Lego? Yes, that's right: the world-famous brand known for its constructions made from small, interlocking plastic bricks, offering infinite possibilities. A revolutionary idea, today it has the added bonus of being an "old-fashioned", fun and educational way of playing, and is far more appropriate for building the minds of young children than video games. It's even something that grown-ups enjoy. The proof: Alberto Landgraf has made it, if not exactly his muse, at least a favourite instrument of his culinary constructions. The Brazilian chef finds himself, once again, in good company. Others before him have paved the way. Similar ideas were taught from textbooks at many avant-garde schools of the last century: for example, in 1951, in his work *Music of Changes*, composer John Cage learnt to subject his compositions to the logic of chance by drawing inspiration from the Chinese divination text the *I Ching*, a milestone of thought dating back to the first millennium BCE, which in English has been translated as *The Book of Changes* or *The Book of Mutations*. And more recently, in 1975, didn't musician Brian Eno and artist Peter Schmidt create Oblique Strategies, a kind of deck of tarot cards with cryptic aphorisms intended to provide prompts in order to break creator's block? Like the godfather of the prepared piano (Cage) and the *maître des cérémonies* of ambient music with its endless evanescent, self-generating musical architectures (Eno), Landgraf adopted the practical concept of Lego as a method of rearrangement. That intuition was brought to life by finding on the internet the very documentary in which "a dad walks into a toy shop with his little son who longs to have a car and a fire truck for his collection. But the father tells him that he has only a little money, not enough to buy both, so the child has to choose which one to take. That was the spark for the shop owner. After closing his shop, he returned home and began thinking about his dream toys. He imagined a shop in which, in the best of all possible worlds, there would be no more unhappy children. Constructions made of bricks that fit one on top of the other, offering almost infinite possibilities for creating shapes such as houses, buildings, cars, bridges, roads, railways, little people and cowboys. And no more having to buy new toys, as you can build and modify them to your liking using the same bricks. A concept of DIY that in those days – and we're talking about the 1930s – was nothing short of brilliant. That's how to make children happy. The blocks, originally made of wood but now made of plastic for practicality, can be used to build whatever you want. They last a lifetime and never wear out. You can dismantle your toy and rebuild it in a different way, expanding and perfecting it by adding more bricks. Or you can invent new shapes using your imagination and only very few new materials are needed. The Lego system works with blocks: you can remove one part, add others, keep the main idea and the overall perimeter but modify the details. It's this process I eventually started using in the kitchen too."

Remove. Move. Exchange. Assemble. Combining different ingredients according to affinity, contrast and similarities. In search of a balance that can result *only* from successful confrontation. It is a question of dialogue, of the mindful overlapping of flavours and textures. Sour with sweet, spicy with salty, bitter with chlorophyll – one thing leads to another. And it is in the games requiring the most concentration that the most beautiful surprises are sometimes hidden. In a sauce, in a broth, in a pâte à choux made in the traditional way with flour, water, butter and sunflower oil. However, by cooking it for a long time over a very low heat – using very little water and almost toasting – the resulting dough plays with the flavour of a pâté à choux, allowing for variation upon variation. Or, when crustaceans are out of season, a reduced stock of shrimp and lobster shells, beaten together as for a choux dough, perhaps with a tiny amount of *soffritto*, can create a mousse-like effect that lends itself to many different dishes. It can also be the base for many sauces for fish, seafood and even meat.

Linguistically, blocks and make-ahead preparations are therefore more than just foundations: they are full-blown narrative word strings that can be applied as and when needed. They can be inherent to ingredients, but also to techniques. For example, fermentations. Not to ferment this or that but to create variations upon variations. To not hesitate or shun foods that are considered taboo. The first person concerned is the chef himself, who discovered, when he was young and inexperienced, that he was prone to a dangerous allergy to eggs. An affliction that could prove fatal if he ate raw or undercooked eggs. "Sunny side up? I can eat them, but only if I cook them in a way that makes the texture almost like rubber. Obviously, I wouldn't inflict that on anyone." But how can he avoid becoming fatally poisoned when his professional duty as a chef dictates that he must taste everything? "While working on techniques suitable for my idea of blocks, I discovered that many things could be done without even going near an egg. Meringues for example. Or a whipped mayonnaise with fish stock. Fermentations are part of the range of preparations always on hand, with a varied repertoire in the fridge. These include a reduced carrot juice and vinegars, of which we have an extensive collection. We never use kefir, only lactic fermentations with tomatoes, raspberries, blueberries and any berries or red fruits available in summer. With barbecued meat, we use an onion

base that serves to bring out the flavour. But if you prepare lamb in the oven, a leg for example, brushing it with a fruit fermentation will set off an umami sensation that is truly unmatched."

We should put Alberto Landgraf at the heart of the action. With just a few tables and a small number of diners, Oteque is a culinary atelier where any acrobatics come naturally and are not performed; where the chef creates a daily menu of exclusive ready-to-eat offerings – an inclusive form of bespoke cuisine. Catering to all needs, to all desires. Alongside the main fare, there are several offshoots that can be incorporated to create subtle customisations. For this chef, the practice of using blocks is not written in stone. It does not aspire to a totality, to a closed worldview, but lends itself to a game of variations, customisations. While he does not lay outright claim to it ("With this block methodology, we can make corrections to a dish in a few minutes and even revise an entire menu from scratch in not much more time than that."), there is something in his versatile responsiveness and the implicit transformative nature of his cooking that has long been common practice in the fields of music and contemporary art. In music, it is remixing and morphing. Nothing is lost; everything is transformed. It is up to the regulars, the philologists of culinary criticism, to track his creative chronology and his evolution as a chef. Who would have suspected that the genesis of a showstopper dish – rock mullet, cashew cream and trout roe – had its roots in a medley of signature dishes from past seasons? Landgraf remembers well a mullet dish that was unanimously declared a hit by everyone, except for one single diner who became the reason for a creative change. "It seems like only yesterday that I was preparing this magnificent mullet with sweet potatoes, roasted barley cream and bone marrow. The dish was hugely popular, yet one evening a diner at Oteque raised an objection: he just couldn't stomach bone marrow. Could I kindly offer him, he asked, something else? Returning to the kitchen, and this is a good example of what I mean by blocks, I offered him again... the same mullet. Replacing just one ingredient – using liver instead of marrow – made the dish both logical and totally different, thanks to the sweet fattiness of the liver. I say logical because it drew a compliment from the diner who admitted that he loved liver. 'I never imagined it could replace the marrow, and in my opinion it's even better!' he exclaimed, surprised at how fast I had satisfied his request. For me, using blocks in this way is a form of mental hygiene and conceptual gymnastics, and enables me to be highly versatile."

A master of improvisation, Landgraf interprets, moves wildly and pirouettes but always falls on his feet. Irreverence goes a long way. And it makes him even better. Take, for example, the buttery, freshly toasted brioche traditionally served with foie gras at the finest French restaurants. ("In my London days, I made so many of those!"). Instead, he serves it with an iconic ingredient in popular food culture: filleted raw sardines with an almost imperceptible amount of chicken liver pâté. "It has the same creamy texture as foie gras, but the combination of the liver and brioche creates an even smoother consistency, which is complemented by the sardines that require an enjoyable amount of chewing." When cooking, one should always be on the alert. To rectify, using anything unexpected to one's advantage. Pork belly, but a smidge too fatty and too hard? Perhaps it no longer lends itself to a cream of caramelised cashew nuts that was its original partner. That cream of Amazonian walnuts can be replaced with another beautiful combination, such as the green, bitter astringency of a parsley dressing, which brings to mind the old expression that says: "To be beautiful, it must be spicy," in the way that opposites attract. A pork cheek – meltingly soft inside and crispy on the outside – goes wonderfully well with it, brightened by that vibrant touch.

"I don't claim to have discovered a new great philosophical system. Simply put, our years of experience with these blocks has enabled us to develop a repertoire of techniques and tricks involving the same basic ingredients, producing ever-different effects. For example, aromatic oils made with dried herbs mixed with various spices come to mind. Or one made with dried mushrooms that works brilliantly with meat: In Brazil, the mushrooms are extraordinary, and we harvest tons of them. I could use mirin, umeboshi and natto, which are traditional Japanese ingredients made from fermented beans. Many people dislike the flavour of natto, which puts your taste limits to the test. But there would be little point in incorporating Japanese ingredients here, in a Brazilian restaurant. I prefer to keep trying, to experiment, to find my own way. I still haven't found good results for making umeboshi, for example, and I've been trying to make it with local plums for seven years already. I tried with ripe ones and also with very unripe ones. But alas, the results have been paltry. I've got many jars of them, but honestly, I couldn't even call them preserved plums. But one day I might be able to do something interesting with them."

Time will tell. Oteque may be a great restaurant, but for us it is above all a container, an incubator, if you like – a term commonly used for startups – of ideas and energy. Alberto Landgraf is not one to spill the beans to the first passer-by. Not even to the highest bidder. Yet the evidence is implicit in the name itself. Exactly: what the hell kind of name is that for a restaurant? Where does it come from, what on earth does Oteque mean? Hey, picture this! Alberto Landgraf grins from ear to ear, all his teeth on show: "It comes from a song by Radiohead, a band I'm a big fan of," he ventures, also admitting – although not to everyone – that he loves Oasis and Coldplay, but hey... "In their album *Kid A*, perhaps their most experimental and radical record, released 25 years ago and still relevant today, there's a song called 'Idioteque'. '*Idio*' in Latin, means singular, personal, and '*teque*' reminds me of the suffix '*teca*' that is found in so many Portuguese words such as *biblio-teca*, *video-teca*, *disco-teca*. It sounds good. In a composite word, it seems to suggest the nature of Oteque: a restaurant where new things and ideas are constantly being brought together, collected and experimented with." Never has an explanation been more descriptive or revealing.

Tuna, fish mayonnaise, caviar
→ p. 134

Shrimp, pirão, pimenta de cheiro
→ p. 136

Squid, shimeji, vegetable cream

→ p. 135

Seabass, fermented tomato
→ p. 137

**Red mullet, parsley, foie gras**
→ p. 138

**Mussels, carrot**
→ p. 139

Grouper, seaweed, caviar
→ p. 140

Duck, apples, jussara cream
→ p. 141

for the LORD thy
God is with thee
whithersoever
thou goest.

# TUNA, FISH MAYONNAISE, CAVIAR → p. 112

- 90g Fish Mayonnaise (page 146)
- 150g caviar (the best you can get)

**For the tuna**

- 600g chutoro tuna
- olive oil
- salt

**Tuna**

Cut the tuna into 3cm-thick slices, season with olive oil and salt and leave to rest at room temperature for 10 minutes. Heat a stainless-steel cooking net until very hot. Using a glove or tongs, sear the tuna. Put the fish mayonnaise in a pastry bag and snip the tip.

**Serve**

Arrange 100g of seasoned tuna in the middle of the plate, pipe the mayonnaise along the top of the tuna and cover the mayonnaise with caviar.

—

**Carbon footprint**

chutoro tuna 74.75%; caviar 22.39%; fish mayonnaise 2.28%; olive oil 0.35%; salt 0.23%

**Total emissions per serving**

1.66kg $CO_2e$

# SQUID, SHIMEJI, VEGETABLE CREAM → p. 119

- chives, finely chopped
- lemon juice, to taste
- drizzle of olive oil
- Porcini Oil (page 146), for drizzling
- Sea Urchin Bottarga (page 147), for grating
- salt, to taste

**For the squid**

- 6 clean squid, with the body separated from the tentacles
- 10g melted pork fat, for brushing
- salt

**For the shimeji mushrooms**

- 100g fresh shimeji mushrooms

**For the vegetable cream**

- 180g Vegetable Base (page 145)
- 150g butter
- 1g xanthan gum
- lemon juice, to taste
- salt, to taste

**Squid**

Cut open the bodies of the squid widthways at the base, clean away the innards and remove the skin. Score the inside of the bodies lightly in a crosshatch pattern. Brush the pork fat over the scored flesh, season with salt and cook over hot embers for 1 minute, then do the same with the tentacles. Be careful not to overcook it, otherwise the squid will get rubbery. Cut the squid bodies thinly into rounds.

**Shimeji mushrooms**

Shred the shimeji to separate the mushrooms from each other and cook for 1 minute over hot embers, constantly turning them and being careful not to let them burn.

**Vegetable cream**

Combine the vegetable base and butter in a saucepan and heat until it boils, then add the xanthan gum and emulsify with a stick blender. Season with salt and lemon juice.

**Finish**

Mix the grilled squid rounds, tentacles and shimeji mushrooms in a bowl and season with the chives, lemon juice, drizzle of olive oil and salt to taste.

**Serve**

Put the seasoned shimeji and squid on the plate and cover with the vegetable cream. Finish with a drizzle of porcini oil and some grated bottarga.

—

**Carbon footprint**

butter 37.52%; porcini oil 15.88%; vegetable base 14.24%; squid 11.2%; olive oil 7.43%; shimeji mushrooms 3.57%; salt 3.47%; pork fat 3.31%; lemon juice 2.06%; sea urchin bottarga 0.89%; xanthan gum 0.39%; chives 0.04%

**Total emissions per serving**

0.23kg $CO_2e$

# SHRIMP, PIRÃO, PIMENTA DE CHEIRO → p. 115

- 18g Pimenta de Cheiro Vinaigrette (page 146)
- 5g Parsley Oil (page 146)

**For the pirão**
- 500g Shrimp Base (page 145)
- 21g cassava flour, sifted
- 150g Raw Cashew Nut Cream (page 144)
- lemon juice, to taste
- salt, to taste

**For the shrimp**
- 200g Shrimp Base (page 145)
- 100g Vegetable Base (page 145)
- 6 fresh shrimp, peeled (80g peeled shrimp per person)

**Pirão**
Put the shrimp base in a saucepan and place over a low heat. Add the cassava flour once it's simmering and blend with a stick blender (over the heat) for 3 minutes. Cook the mixture over a low heat for 2 hours, mixing with the stick blender every 15 minutes, then add the raw cashew nut cream and cook for another 1 hour, still mixing it with the stick blender every 15 minutes. Strain through a chinois and season with salt and lemon juice.

**Shrimp**
Combine the shrimp base and vegetable base in a saucepan and reduce over a medium heat to a thin glaze. Let the fresh shrimp come to room temperature, then grill one side over hot embers for 40 seconds. Brush the glaze on the ungrilled side and return to the embers glazed side down for 40 seconds.

**Finish**
Strain 1 teaspoon of the pimenta de cheiro vinaigrette and mix it with the parsley oil.

**Serve**
Place 2 tablespoons of pirão in the middle of the plate. Place the grilled shrimp on one side of the plate and on the other side place 1 teaspoon of the mixture of pimenta de cheiro vinaigrette.

—

**Carbon footprint**
shrimp 61.21%; shrimp base 24.69%; raw cashew nut cream 10.39%; salt 1.76%; vegetable base 1.08%; parsley oil 0.37%; pimenta de cheiro vinaigrette 0.29%; cassava flour 0.12%; lemon juice 0.08%
**Total emissions per serving**
1.7kg $CO_2e$

# SEABASS, FERMENTED TOMATO → p. 121

- Kombu Oil (page 146), for drizzling
- Fermented Tomato Base (page 147), reduced to a thin glaze
- olive oil, for drizzling
- mizuna leaves, to garnish

**For the dried tomatoes**
- 50 yellow and red sweet grape tomatoes (or any variety you can find)
- olive oil, for drizzling
- sugar, to taste
- salt, to taste

**For tomato paste**
- 200g dried tomatoes (above)
- 4 anchovy fillets in oil
- olive oil, for drizzling

**For the seabass**
- 100g fine sea salt
- 1kg water
- 1 seabass, cleaned, gutted and separated into loins (skinless)

**Dried tomatoes**
Score an 'x' in the bottom of each tomato and blanch them in boiling water, then peel away the skin. Spread them out on a baking tray and season each one with a drizzle of olive oil and a pinch each of salt and sugar. Dehydrate in the oven at 85°C (185°F) for 1–2 hours until completely dry. Reserve the dried tomatoes with a coating of olive oil in a vacuum bag sealed under total vacuum.

**Tomato paste**
Mince all the dried tomatoes with the anchovy fillets using the tip of a knife to make a tomato paste. Add a drizzle of olive oil and keep in the refrigerator until ready to serve.

**Seabass**
Dissolve the fine salt in the water in a 10cm-deep 1/3 gastro to make a brine. Immerse the seabass loins for 4 minutes. Drain the brine, cut the loin into 2.5mm-thick slices and keep in the refrigerator until ready to serve.

**Finish**
Add a drizzle of kombu oil to the tomato paste and combine.

**Serve**
Place 2 seabass slices in the middle of the plate and brush the reduced fermented tomato on each one. Shape a quenelle of tomato paste on top, in the middle, and place 4 dried tomatoes around. Finish with a drizzle of kombu oil around the seabass and some mizuna leaves.

—

**Carbon footprint**
seabass 69.09%; salt 15.32%; olive oil 7.16%; sweet grape tomatoes 4.26%; anchovies 3.09%; kombu oil 0.49%; sugar 0.39%; water 0.14%; fermented tomato base 0.03%; mizuna leaves 0.03%
**Total emissions per serving**
1.29kg $CO_2e$

# RED MULLET, PARSLEY, FOIE GRAS → p. 122

- 6 tablespoons Parsley Emulsion (page 147), in a squeezy bottle
- 6 teaspoons trout roe
- 6 small radishes, cut into quarters
- wood sorrel leaves, to garnish

**For the red mullet**

- 100g fine sea salt, plus extra to taste
- 1kg water
- 3 red mullets, scaled and portioned into 6 fillets (with the skin intact)
- olive oil, for brushing

**For the foie gras emulsion**

- 1 small shallot, cut into 1mm cubes
- olive oil, for drizzling
- 40g Cognac (the best you can get)
- 80g Vegetable Base (page 145)
- 120g Chicken Wings Base (page 145)
- 800g raw foie gras, cut into 3cm cubes
- organic apple cider vinegar, to taste
- salt, to taste

**Red mullet**

Dissolve the fine salt in the water in a 10cm-deep 1/3 gastro to make a brine and immerse the red mullet fillets in the brine for 5 minutes. Drain the brine and dry the fillets with a paper towel. Place them on a grill tray skin side up, brush the skins with olive oil, season with salt and grill under a salamander grill set at high heat for 2 minutes 30 seconds, then remove and let them rest at room temperature.

**Foie gras emulsion**

Sweat the shallot in a saucepan with a drizzle of olive oil over a medium heat until softened but not browned. Pour in the Cognac and let it reduce until the pan is almost dry, then add the vegetable and the chicken bases. Bring to the boil, then add the foie gras cubes, a few at a time, blending with a stick blender to emulsify the mixture (with the pan still over the heat). Pass the emulsion through a chinois and season with apple vinegar and salt.

**Serve**

Put a red mullet fillet on the centre of the plate, skin side up. Place 1 tablespoon of foie gras emulsion on one side of the fillet, and on the other side 1 tablespoon of parsley emulsion. Finish with 1 teaspoon of trout roe, sliced radishes and wood sorrel leaves.

—

**Carbon footprint**

foie gras 84.68%; trout roe 5.21%; red mullets 4.63%; salt 2.68%; Cognac 1.4%; vegetable base 0.36%; olive oil 0.31%; chicken wings base 0.3%; radishes 0.22%; parsley emulsion 0.12%; apple vinegar 0.03%; water 0.02%; shallot 0.02%; wood sorrel leaves 0.02%

**Total emissions per serving**

7.59kg $CO_2e$

# MUSSELS, CARROT → p. 124

- 6 slices (6 x 3cm) of brioche, or any soft bread, to serve

**For the thyme oil**
- 2 bunches of thyme
- 200g rapeseed oil

**For the mussels**
- olive oil, for drizzling
- 2kg mussels in their shells
- 200g white wine
- 1 onion, quartered

**For the carrot sauce**
- 400g carrot juice, made fresh with a juice extractor
- 300g reserved mussel broth (see above)
- 50g white wine vinegar
- 2g salt

**Thyme oil**
Dry the thyme sprigs in the microwave in 30-second bursts until they turn completely dry. Put them in a Thermomix with the rapeseed oil and blend for 1 minute at high speed. Decant into a muslin-lined chinois and leave to strain overnight.

**Mussels**
Drizzle some olive oil into a large saucepan over a high heat, add the mussels, add the white wine and the onion, cover the pan with a lid and cook for 3 minutes. Strain through a chinois and reserve the liquid for the carrot sauce. Release the mussels from their shells and grill over hot embers for 90 seconds on each side just before serving.

**Carrot sauce**
Boil the carrot juice in a saucepan until foam forms, then strain through a muslin-lined chinois to remove the foam. Reduce the juice to 300g in a saucepan, then mix in the mussel broth and vinegar and season with the salt.

**Serve**
Place one brioche slice in the middle of the plate and place 4 mussels on top. Pour the carrot sauce around and finish with thyme oil drops.

—

**Carbon footprint**
rapeseed oil 23.04%; mussels 19.47%; white wine 17.28%; white wine vinegar 16.71%; olive oil 9.32%; brioche 7.04%; carrot juice 4.38%; onion 1.41%; thyme 0.94%; salt 0.4%
**Total emissions per serving**
0.62kg $CO_2$e

# GROUPER, SEAWEED, CAVIAR → p. 125

**For the grouper**

- 100g fine sea salt
- 1kg water
- 1 grouper, cleaned, gutted and separated into loins

**For the seaweed vinaigrette**

- 200g Vegetable Base (page 145)
- squeeze of lemon juice, to taste
- 50g Kombu Oil (page 146), to taste
- chives, finely chopped, to taste
- salt, to taste

**To serve**

- 6 teaspoons caviar (the best you can get)
- 10g toasted pine nuts
- elderflowers, to garnish

**Grouper**

Dissolve the fine salt in the water in a 15cm-deep 1/2 gastro to make a brine and immerse the grouper loin in the brine for 4 minutes. Drain the brine, thinly slice the loin, and keep in the refrigerator until ready to serve.

**Seaweed vinaigrette**

Simmer the vegetable base in a saucepan until it reduces by half, then let it cool at room temperature. Season to taste with the lemon juice, kombu oil, salt and chives.

**Serve**

Place 3 slices of grouper in the middle of the plate, cover with 2 tablespoons of the seaweed vinaigrette and top with a teaspoon of caviar. Finish with the pine nuts and elderflowers.

—

**Carbon footprint**

grouper 79.91%; salt 8.66%; kombu oil 4.75%; caviar 3.39%; vegetable base 1.68%; pine nuts 1.4%; lemon juice 0.09%; water 0.08%; elderflowers 0.03%; chives 0.01%

**Total emissions per serving**

2.2kg $CO_2$e

# DUCK, APPLES, JUSSARA CREAM → p. 129

- dwarf pellitory leaves, to garnish

**For the duck**
- 2 duck breasts, cleaned
- salt, to taste

**For the apples**
- 2 Fuji apples
- butter, to taste

**For the jussara cream**
- drizzle of olive oil
- ½ onion, chopped
- 1 garlic clove, chopped
- 500g fresh jussara pulp
- 100g Beef Shin Base (page 144)
- 15g organic apple cider vinegar
- salt, to taste

**Duck**
Preheat the oven to 200°C (392°F). With the duck at room temperature, score the skin and sprinkle with salt to taste. Heat an ovenproof frying pan over a high heat, place the duck breasts skin side down in the pan and let the fat render until the skin caramelizes. Turn and sear on the other side, then transfer to the oven and cook for 5 minutes. Remove and let rest at room temperature before slicing to serve.

**Apples**
Cut the apples into 5mm-thick triangles and sear on both sides in a frying pan over a low heat in some butter for 10 minutes until caramelized.

**Jussara cream**
Heat the olive oil in a frying pan over a medium heat, add the onion and garlic and cook until softened, then add the jussara pulp and bring to the boil. Add the beef shin base and apple cider vinegar, season with salt and bring to the boil. Blend with a stick blender and strain through a tamis.

**Serve**
Place 1 tablespoon of jussara cream on the middle of the place. Slice each duck breast and place slices on either side of the cream. Place the caramelized apple slices around the duck and garnish with dwarf pellitory leaves.

—

**Carbon footprint**
duck breast 51.39%; beef shin base 41.51%; jussara 27.56%; Fuji apples 1.65%; salt 0.9%; onion 0.23%; apple cider vinegar 0.2%; butter 0.15%; garlic 0.05%; dwarf pellitory leaves 0.02%; olive oil 0.39%
**Total emissions per serving**
2.54kg $CO_2e$

# RAW CASHEW NUT CREAM

- 300g cashew nuts
- 200g room-temperature water
- 100g rapeseed oil
- 65g lemon juice
- salt, to taste

Blend the cashew nuts in a Thermomix at high speed until finely ground. Change the speed setting to 4 and gradually add the water first, then the rapeseed oil. Blend for 5 minutes on setting 7, then transfer the mixture to a bowl, cover with cling film (making sure the film is in contact with the surface of the cream) and let it cool down in the refrigerator. Once cold, add the lemon juice, and season with salt to taste. Keep in the refrigerator.

# CARAMELIZED BRAZIL NUTS

- 1kg raw Brazil nuts
- 100g molasses
- 10g salt

Mix all the ingredients together in a bowl until all the nuts are evenly coated with the molasses. Put the nuts, evenly distributed, in a vacuum bag and seal under full vacuum. Remove from the bag and dehydrate in a dehydrator at 60°C (140°F) for 20 days. Once the nuts are caramelized, store in the refrigerator in the bag.

# CARAMELIZED BRAZIL NUT MILK

- 300g Caramelized Brazil Nuts (above)
- 300g room-temperature water
- 100g rapeseed oil
- 1g xanthan gum

Blend the nuts and water in a Thermomix, briefly, at high speed. Transfer to the refrigerator overnight, then blend the mixture in the Thermomix again for 2 minutes at high speed. Strain through a muslin-lined chinois, return to the blender and gradually add the rapeseed oil with the blender running. Finally, mix in the xanthan gum. Store in a squeezy bottle.

# BRAZIL NUT MILK

- 300g Brazil nuts
- 300g room-temperature water
- 100g rapeseed oil
- 5g xanthan gum
- pinch of salt

Blend the nuts and water in a Thermomix, briefly, at high speed. Transfer to the refrigerator overnight, then blend the mixture in the Thermomix again for 2 minutes at high speed. Strain through a muslin-lined chinois, return to the blender and gradually add the oil and xanthan gum.

# PORK SPINE BROTH

- 10kg pork spine, cut into shorter lengths
- 800g onions, roughly chopped
- 400g carrots, roughly chopped
- 600g leeks, trimmed and washed, roughly chopped
- 15kg water
- 40g dried shiitake mushrooms
- 40g kombu
- 20g thyme sprigs

Preheat the oven to 200°C (392°F). Roast the pork spine in the oven for 15 minutes on a roasting tray. Put the roasted spine and the vegetables in a large stock pot with the water, dried shiitake, kombu and thyme and cook over a low heat for 10 hours. Strain through a chinois and chill in the refrigerator overnight. Once cold, remove all the solidified fat on top. Boil the broth, then strain it through a muslin and leave to cool.

# PORK NECK BASE

- 12kg pork neck, cut into 7cm cubes
- 15kg water
- 800g onions, roughly chopped
- 600g leeks, roughly chopped
- 400g carrots, roughly chopped
- 40g kombu
- 40g dried shiitake mushrooms
- 20g thyme sprigs

Put the pork neck in a large stock pot, cover with water and bring to the boil. When a foam forms on the surface, drain the water and wash the meat under running water. Return the pork neck to the pot and add enough water to cover (the 15kg should be enough), then add all the vegetables, with the kombu, shiitake and thyme. Simmer over a medium heat for 18 hours. Strain to remove the solids, then strain again through a muslin-lined chinois. Chill in the refrigerator overnight. Once cold, remove all the solidified fat on top.

# BEEF SHIN BASE

- 12kg beef shin, cut into 7cm cubes
- 15kg water
- 800g onions, roughly chopped
- 600g leeks, roughly chopped
- 400g carrots, roughly chopped
- 40g kombu
- 40g dried shiitake mushrooms
- 20g thyme sprigs

Put the beef in a large stock pot, cover with water and bring to the boil. When a foam forms on the surface, drain the water and wash the meat under running water. Return the shin to the pot and add enough water to cover (the 15kg should be enough), then add all the vegetables, with the kombu, shiitake and thyme. Simmer over a medium heat for 18 hours. Strain to remove the solids, then strain again through a muslin-lined chinois. Chill in the refrigerator overnight. Once cold, remove all the solidified fat on top.

## CHICKEN WINGS BASE

- 12kg chicken wings
- 15kg water
- 800g onions, roughly chopped
- 600g leeks, roughly chopped
- 400g carrots, roughly chopped
- 40g dried shiitake mushrooms
- 40g kombu
- 20g thyme

Preheat the oven to 200°C (392°F). Roast the chicken wings on a roasting tray in the oven for 25 minutes, until caramelized. Put all the ingredients, including the roasted chicken wings, in a large stock pot and simmer over a medium heat for 18 hours. Strain to remove the solids, then strain again through a muslin-lined chinois. Chill in the refrigerator overnight. Once cold, remove all the solidified fat on top.

## VEGETABLE BASE

- 260g onions, roughly chopped
- 460g carrots, roughly chopped
- 260g leeks, roughly chopped
- 1kg water
- 40g dried shiitake mushrooms
- 40g kombu
- 20g thyme sprigs

Put all the vegetables in a vacuum bag with the water, dried shiitake, kombu and thyme, seal under full vacuum and cook in a water bath at 85°C (185°F) for 2 hours. Strain through a chinois to remove the solids.

## FISH BASE

- 5kg fish head (gills removed), trims and fish bones
- 12kg water
- 800g onions, roughly chopped
- 600g leeks, roughly chopped
- 40g dried shiitake mushrooms
- 20g kombu

Put the fish head, trims and bones in a container, cover with water, and leave in the refrigerator overnight, to remove excess blood. The next day, put the drained fish bones, heads and trims in a large stock pot, add the 12kg water, onions, leeks, dried shiitake and kombu and simmer over a low heat for 4 hours. Strain through a chinois and chill in the refrigerator overnight. Once cold, remove all the solidified fat on top. Boil the base, then strain it through a muslin-lined chinois and leave to cool.

## SHRIMP BASE

- 5kg shrimp heads and shells
- 12kg water
- 800g onions, roughly chopped
- 600g leeks, roughly chopped
- 300g tomatoes, roughly chopped
- 40g dried shiitake mushrooms
- 20g kombu

In a large stock pot, sauté the shrimp heads and shells until caramelized. Add the water, onions, leeks, tomatoes, dried shiitake and kombu and simmer over a low heat for 3 hours. Strain through a muslin-lined chinois and leave to cool.

## PICKLED SHALLOTS

- 100g water
- 100g white vinegar
- 20g salt
- 10g sugar
- 150g shallots, peeled and halved

Mix the water, vinegar, salt and sugar in a saucepan and heat until boiling. Add the shallots to the boiling mixture, turn off the heat and let it sit for 2 minutes. Transfer the mixture to a bowl placed over an ice bath to cool. Store in a sterilized glass jar or vacuum bag in your refrigerator for 2 hours.

## CURED PORK BELLY

- 100g molasses
- 2kg deboned pork belly
- 450g salt
- 225g sugar
- 50g curing salt
- 10g black pepper, freshly ground
- 3 bay leaves
- bunch of thyme sprigs
- grated zest of 1 orange
- grated zest of 1 lemon

Rub the molasses all over the pork belly. Combine the salt, sugar, curing salt, black pepper, bay leaves, thyme and the lemon and orange zests in a bowl and cover the belly with the mixture. Put it in a shallow tray, cover with cling film and chill in the refrigerator for 24 hours. Wash the belly, dry with a paper towel and hang it in a cured meat refrigerator for 40–45 days. Slice thinly lengthways using a slicer machine, to serve.

## MUSHROOM VINAIGRETTE

- 2kg olive oil (or enough to cover), plus a drizzle for frying
- 300g white button mushrooms, finely chopped
- 300g fresh porcini mushrooms, finely chopped
- 300g fresh shiitake mushrooms, finely chopped
- 200g shallots, finely chopped
- bunch of thyme sprigs
- 400g balsamic vinegar
- salt, to taste

Heat the drizzle of olive oil in a frying pan over a high heat, add all the mushrooms and the shallots and cook for 5 minutes until caramelized. Put the cooked mushrooms, shallots and thyme in a clean jar, cover with the olive oil, seal the jar with cling film and let it rest in the refrigerator for 20 days. Remove the thyme, blend the mixture with a stick blender until finely ground, then season with salt and the balsamic vinegar. Store in a sealed container in the refrigerator.

# PIMENTA DE CHEIRO VINAIGRETTE

- 100g water
- 100g white vinegar
- 20g salt
- 10g sugar
- 150g pimenta de cheiro, halved and deseeded

Put the water, vinegar, salt and sugar in a saucepan and heat until boiling. Add the pimenta de cheiro to the boiling mixture, then turn off the heat, cover with a lid and let it sit for 3 minutes to infuse. Pour the mixture into a bowl set over an ice bath. Cut the pimenta de cheiro into small brunoise once the mixture is cool, then transfer the pimenta and vinegary liquid to a sterilized glass jar. Store in the refrigerator.

# SHIITAKE CONFIT

- 150g fresh shiitake mushrooms, cut into 3mm cubes
- 100g olive oil, plus extra for drizzling

Preheat a steam oven (100% steam) to 90°C (194°F). Heat a drizzle of olive oil in a frying pan over a high heat, add the shiitake and sauté for 3 minutes until lightly browned. Put the mushrooms in a vacuum bag with the 100g olive oil, seal under full vacuum and cook in the steam oven for 25 minutes. Let it cool to room temperature and keep in the refrigerator overnight before using.

# MUSHROOM POWDER

- 200g dried shiitake mushrooms
- 200g dried porcini mushrooms

Blend the dried mushrooms in a Thermomix at high speed for 2 minutes, until they form a powder.

# PORCINI OIL

- 100g dried ceps
- 100g rapeseed oil or grapeseed oil

Preheat a steam oven (100% steam) to 100°C (212°F). Combine the dried ceps with the oil in a vacuum bag, seal under full vacuum and cook in the steam oven for 2 hours. Strain through a muslin-lined chinois, pour into a small squeezy bottle and keep refrigerated.

# KOMBU OIL

- 100g dried kombu
- 100g rapeseed oil or grapeseed oil

Preheat a steam oven (100% steam) to 100°C (212°F). Combine the dried kombu with the oil in a vacuum bag, seal under full vacuum and cook in the steam oven for 2 hours. Strain through a muslin-lined chinois, pour into a small squeezy bottle and keep refrigerated.

# PIMENTA BIQUINHO OIL

- 1kg pimenta biquinho, stems removed
- 400g rapeseed oil

Dehydrate the pimenta biquinho at 60°C (140°F) for 24 hours. Blend all the dehydrated pimentas in a Thermomix at high speed until they form a powder. Heat the rapeseed oil in a pan or pot to 80°C (176°F) – this will take about 3 minutes – then add the pimenta biquinho powder. Turn off the heat and let it rest in the pan until it reaches room temperature to infuse all the flavours. Strain through a muslin-lined chinois, pour into a small squeezy bottle and keep refrigerated.

# PARSLEY OIL

- 300g parsley leaves
- 300g grapeseed oil

Blend the parsley and oil in a Thermomix at high speed for 8 minutes until it reaches 75°C (167°F). Strain through a muslin-lined chinois and store in a sealed container.

# FISH MAYONNAISE

- 600g Fish Base (page 145)
- 600g rapeseed oil
- lemon juice, to taste
- salt, to taste

Reduce the fish base in a saucepan by two-thirds, until you have 200g. Let it cool in the refrigerator until it has a gelatinous consistency. Blend it in a Thermomix at high speed and gradually add the rapeseed oil to emulsify. Season with salt and lemon juice, to taste.

# SIMPLE SYRUP

- 200g sugar
- 200g water

Put the sugar and water in a saucepan, place over a low heat, then simmer until the sugar dissolves. Let it cool at room temperature and store in a sealed container in the refrigerator.

# DRIED YEAST

- 30g fresh yeast

Break the yeast into crumbs. Line a 1.5cm-deep gastro with parchment paper, spread the crumbs over the paper-lined gastro and bake in a dry oven at 70°C (158°F) for 1 hour. Store in a sealed container.

# PARSLEY EMULSION

- 50g parsley, leaves picked
- 400g organic Greek yogurt
- 40g rapeseed oil
- 2g xanthan gum

Put the parsley leaves and yogurt in a food processor and blend to a smooth cream. Pass through a tamis, then froth with a stick blender while gradually adding the rapeseed oil until a smooth, velvety texture is achieved. Stabilize with the xanthan at the end. Pour into a squeezy bottle and keep refrigerated.

# SEA URCHIN BOTTARGA

- 100g fine sea salt
- 1kg water
- 400g sea urchin roe

Dissolve the fine salt in the water in a 10cm-deep 1/3 gastro to make a brine, add the sea urchin roe and brine for 24 hours in the refrigerator. Drain the brine, divide the roe in half and place each half on a sheet of non-stick parchment paper – spin tightly to make 2 rolls, securing or tying the ends to seal. Place in a dehydrator at 60°C (140°F) for 10 hours. Remove the paper and reshape the roll. Return the rolls (with the paper) to the dehydrator for another 48 hours, at the same temperature. Reshape the roll again and return to the dehydrator for another 24–48 hours until it becomes firm. To store, place in a vacuum bag, seal under full vacuum, then store in a dry room for up to 3 months.

# JUNIPER POWDER

- 200g dried juniper berries

Blend the berries in a Thermomix at high speed until they form a powder. Store in a sealed container at room temperature.

# FERMENTED TOMATO (POWDER AND BASE)

**For the tomato powder**
- 1.2kg tomatoes, cut into quarters
- 24g salt

**For the tomato base**
- 1kg fermented tomato water (see below)
- 260g onions, roughly chopped
- 460g carrots, roughly chopped
- 260g leeks, trimmed, washed and roughly chopped
- 20g dried shiitake mushrooms
- 20g kombu
- 10g thyme sprigs

**Tomato powder**
Put the quartered tomatoes and salt in a vacuum bag and seal under full vacuum. Leave the bag at room temperature to ferment until the bag inflates – this usually takes 5 days. Open the bag, then strain the contents through muslin to separate the liquid from the solids. The liquid is the fermented tomato water that you will use in the second recipe below. Squeeze the solids to yield as much liquid as possible. Reserve the solids to make the tomato powder. Spread the solid fermented tomato on a Silpat and dehydrate in a dehydrator at 60°C (140°F) for 24 hours. Blitz in a food processor at high speed until it forms a powder. Store in a sealed container at room temperature.

**Tomato base**
Preheat a steam oven (100% steam) to 85°C (185°F). Combine the fermented tomato water, onions, carrots, leeks, dried shiitake, kombu and thyme in a vacuum bag, seal under full vacuum and cook in the steam oven for 2 hours. Strain through a chinois. Keep in a bag or a sealed jar in the refrigerator.

# SHIO KOMBU (POWDER AND PARTICLES)

**For the powder**
- 10g shoyu
- 5g mirin (or the best Japanese sweet white wine you can get)
- 5g rice vinegar
- 3g sugar
- 15g kombu, washed and cut into strips

**For the particles**
- 5g salt
- 3g sugar

**Powder**
Preheat the oven to 100°C (121°F). Put all the measured liquids and the sugar in a saucepan and boil to dissolve. Add the kombu to the pan, reduce the heat and cook for 5 minutes, until the liquid dries. Put the kombu on a Silpat and bake it in the oven for 30–40 minutes until it is dehydrated. Keep an eye on it.

**Particles**
Combine the salt and sugar, then place in a bag with the dehydrated kombu. Give the bag a shake to make sure the entire surface of the kombu pieces is covered with the mixture. Blend the coated kombu in a coffee grinder and sift to separate the powder from the larger particles – both parts of the shio kombu will be used in recipes.

# 04

# LEADERSHIP

Natural-born leaders are, of course, born. But you can also gradually become a natural leader. It is a question of predisposition, of mental agility. Of the apprenticeship of life being conceived as a common good. No ruler-like posturing, no rabble-rousing: Alberto Landgraf is fully aware of how blurred the line is between decisive lucidity and sterile self-satisfaction. Love thy neighbour almost as thyself: "Love means never having to say you are sorry," (Erich Segal, 1969). This concise chapter is proof of that, and is a component block of Landgraf's "sociobiography", made up of an interlude, epilogue and epigraph. Here, this chef lays bare the extent to which his methodology owes to an innate spirit of excellence and competitive drive, but with a fundamental focus on sharing. It was his mother who urged the then footballer with quicksilver in his veins to better channel and focus his energy. "For my mother, who taught English and Portuguese, teaching was a vocation. After spending a lifetime in the classroom, she retired, but after just a few months, she started teaching again, this time the language of Braille to the visually impaired. She used to tell me that if I wanted to be a leader – although back then she was mainly referring to sport and my involvement in football and volleyball – I would have to take the initiative. But then she'd immediately add that, whatever I decided to do at school or in life or at work, if I wanted to be a champion – not just number one but a true leader – I had to be able to pass on my knowledge and share my experience with others. I was on the right track, I was always top of the class at school, I always took the initiative for group science projects, I never shied away from anything. Those words have always stayed with me. In particular when, years later I had to reflect on my role as a head chef and business manager."

Chef patron is not just a label. In Landgraf's case, it is a *Weltanschauung*. Or, translating the term from German into the sensitive perspective of that young Brazilian: a vision, a philosophy of life. To not stumble again or make the same mistakes, the same conditioned reflexes – either his own or those of the profession – of his past experiences. Still wet behind the ears, Landgraf was using a wide aperture for maximum depth of field. He failed to grasp the culture of tacit agreement and the ironclad, unchanging rules of conduct that rendered individual action impossible in a group environment. Between Marx's theory of alienation regarding assembly lines – let's face it, aren't all these chefs and cooks nowadays arranging plate after plate of food for delocalised groups the latest and ultimate incarnation of this? – and the spirit of free enterprise, Landgraf sought a third way right from the outset. One based on observation, reflecting better organisation. "Back then, in the early 2000s, before Instagram, the flow of ideas and snippets of life were confined to the kitchen, where the boss's word was unquestioned and was law. The system was set in stone; the dishes themselves seemed to pour down from above – a pyramidal position of power where criticism had no place. But deep inside, I felt that leadership was needed. But in a less strict, totally different way."

Of a new spirit of democracy in the kitchen. Because the weight of creation, like management, does not rest on the shoulders of a single individual. Autarky is a useless dream even in the case of a sushi-only chef facing a few customers on the other side of the counter. Withstand, evolve – hold, yes, of course, but for the long haul, for a long-term project that involves the transmission of craftsmanship, of passing on a mindset. And it raises the question of legacy. True great leaders are those who know how to form teams, motivate their troops, know how to leave something of themselves behind. In hindsight, Landgraf's mentors, and one in particular, knew how to do this. When you think of Gordon Ramsay, you also think of his former protégés, such as Clare Smyth, Angela Hartnett, Jason Atherton and Aidan Byrne: they have their own sensibilities and personalities, yet they still perpetuate the glories of modern British cuisine. Our legacy could claim, in the manner of the eponymous Swedish design brand: a clear evolution of avant-garde thinking reconnecting with its origins. Oteque, in Rio, a place of memory in the present, an agora of public emulation: "A true leader is by definition not just a great chef to be admired or feared. They are someone able to involve thirty, forty or fifty other people around them, all from different social backgrounds, nationalities and experiences. Transmission is carried out through words, through gestures, through the examples everyone is required to follow. While teaching how to cook ingredients, frying fish, cleaning vegetables and fermenting are important, what seems to me to be far more important is stoking a person's inner fire – their motivation to grow and continue to evolve – in more fruitful ways. It's about them making their own the experiences that will one day be necessary when they feel ready to open their own restaurant," reiterates the head of this motley crew, who sees himself less as a leader than as a guide: a master director of ubiquity, moving between the stalls and proscenium, at the helm of a mise en scène involving everyone's participation and the strict observance of minute gestures and repetitions from a script that is neither set in stone nor a free-for-all. Improvisation takes a back seat when cooking "à la minute" – it's normal: we're in the kitchen! – as there is a general observance of a protocol from which each person must tap into in the interest of all. "Boastful or not, we have all heard of certain chefs who, at the end of the service, rummage through the rubbish bin to see what has been thrown away, how much was wasted, discarded. I understand them, but how can we share their attitude? By training mentally. Despite my analytical attitude to everything, being a control freak doesn't suit me at all. Pedagogy, on the other hand, does. What I teach, particularly to younger people, is that small things result in big projects. Ignoring waste, apart from the immediate loss, when added up sitting after sitting, is significant when it comes to a profit and loss statement, and is the wrong mental attitude to have. Common sense, also motivated by an ethic of sustainability and consistency, implies that there is a common direction. It's not just the logical rooting out of waste and the utilisation of every part of an animal – we buy lamb, beef and pork from our most trusted suppliers, not just the best cuts, but the whole creature. Between one dish and another, the different cuts are prepared in many diverse ways, and little or nothing is thrown away in the end; we even use the bones to make stock. It dictates the very tempo of the activities in a restaurant like ours. Metaphorically speaking, as head of operations, I play the same role as the captain of a boat, setting the rhythm that the front-of-house and kitchen must follow. They have to keep up with me without missing a beat, respecting the exact way I want the work, the basics, cleanliness and speed to be. I don't like monitoring. That's why I try to offer all the tools for taking the initiative. It's group work, but each individual counts. I could draw up a list of things that in my eyes are fundamental, and first and foremost would be respect for everyone. Nicknames are banned at Oteque. We work with kindness and courtesy, and as there is no music, our concentration is enhanced. Accountability is shared, circular. When we prepare our staff meals, we do it as meticulously as if we were cooking for our customers. A true leader is the one who knows how to offer tools of expression to their loyal assistants."

With his enlightened gaze, Alberto Landgraf ponders, answers and draws conclusions, dialectically examining each piece of his mental construction indefinitely. Because they are nourished by observation, the answers often come before the questions themselves. He gives examples galore, making diagrams and mathematical equations. The omnivore of knowledge that he is, as well as a great lover of reliable cars and an avid poker player, he brought out his wild card, even bringing up

Toyota, a car manufacturer that developed the revolutionary 5S model in the immediate post-war period, calling it "a system to make production lines operational."

We confess that at this point we weren't following Landgraf. Not being "au fait" with automotive metaphors, we knew little to nothing about the 5S system. But a quick search was enough to confirm what he said: specifically, it was a concept registered by Toyota aimed at optimising the workspace, decreasing waste and increasing quality and safety. A manufacturing and organisational plan that revolves around five main points. The five principles – five, lo and behold, like the five principles that underpin this book and all of Oteque's activities – all begin with the letter S in Japanese, and could be translated as: sort, set in order, shine, standardise and sustain. These five Gordian knots, when applied to the day-to-day business of a kitchen, strip a destination restaurant of its signature nomenclature to instead initiate a fruitful dialogue with the idea of management.

Permit me a quirky digression. I was astonished to find a distant echo of philosopher Martin Heidegger's exhortation to his students at the University of Freiburg in Alberto Landgraf's words when he addresses the topic of leadership. This echo is found in Heidegger's famous, and still poorly understood, The Rector's Address of 1933. A speech that focused on the mission of philosophy and scientific research, which put the fundamental role of leadership on the table. Here, briefly, is one of his final observations: "All leading must grant the body of followers its own strength. All following, however, bears resistance within itself."

Following a particular leader is therefore to put oneself at risk. To create a blockade around a common project. Resisting stasis and opposing the dominance of technique and praxis by rephrasing familiar phrases. It is about inventing, creating and probing new spaces for reflection; trusting in the other, in their autonomy; conveying formative thoughts and experiences. This Brazilian chef knows something about that, and is inclined to make Oteque a utopian business venture as never before. And because of his obvious ambitions, a leading restaurant in its field. A university of life for these times of confused thinking. "We know how difficult it is to find meaning in what you do if you don't have a broader vision. That's why I spend a lot of time with the youngsters in the team. I generally choose people without much training because they're more receptive to being taught. And, therefore, more responsive. As with Toyota's 5S system, it is a question of training, of organisation, so that the work to be done runs as smoothly as possible. And it is, humanly speaking, also the most respectful you could come up with. Starting with the seemingly most insignificant things: if you're finished with the salt, put it back in its place. Never leave things in a mess, put back anything you don't need in order to make the work of others easier. Respect and consideration are key words that I always repeat to the team members when we talk every day, and I ask them for their impressions. We share the same principles of ethics and proper behaviour at every level."

This is a long-term pedagogical process that requires commitment and a moral contract from both sides. Simply doing a stint at Oteque just to add a prestigious reference to your CV makes no sense. You don't go there to work in isolation, you go to commit to a group project for at least one or two years – long enough to establish yourself. While some throw themselves in at the deep end and perhaps give up shortly afterwards, many others arrive without too many expectations, gradually get to grips with the situation and the creative organisation, and end up staying for about five years. "Many, although ready to fly the nest, become full members of the family and simply don't want to leave. I'm happy, because it means we've succeeded in making Oteque a truly healthy and creative habitat, where people live and work well together, where participation is encouraged."

In doing this, Landgraf is attracting, training and awakening possible talents that lie dormant. Those under his tutelage follow a school of thought or a style of leadership, putting their own spin on it. That friction and personal "resistance" is their contribution and their precious ever-evolving experience, which implies the true passing of the torch: access to a collective dimension of creative co-participation. Others have already walked the same arduous path. Landgraf remarks on René Redzepi's twenty years of work at Noma: "A true leader," he says, recalling the intense, indelible, formative months he spent in that Copenhagen kitchen after closing Epice in São Paulo and before opening Oteque in Rio de Janeiro. "You just have to witness the energy and commitment of everyone from first thing in the morning until late at night, or even attend the briefing just before each sitting, to see all the energy René uses to galvanise the collective spirit of the team." As a somewhat zen-like leader, Landgraf is no less of an unconventional educator. He has his own methods for refining strategies, one tactic at a time. In fact, he claims to have validated certain choices based on eight years of experience. "Ninety per cent of the staff are first-timers, sponges ready to absorb and share our knowledge. I make it a point of honour for the staff in the dining room to be the youngest members of the local community, who have no experience. They come from the countryside and the outskirts, and are complete novices. Which means they aren't blinkered. Even those who have never experienced a restaurant like ours before, or who have never heard of fine dining or tasting menus, gradually adopt our standards. We show them what to do, how to behave and examine different situations. We pay for English courses, as we have a great number of customers from all over the world. We also organise wine initiation classes and coffee tastings, where we explain the nature of coffee, its different qualities and the harvesting and fermentation processes. We not only offer them all the means necessary to understand our work and our mission, but we do our utmost to provide the essential tools for them to integrate, learn and move forwards. Full health insurance is also included, as is accommodation with all mod cons in a flat across the street, just a stone's throw from the restaurant."

Treat your neighbour as you would treat thyself. It is the secret of the common agreement. In a country where the average monthly salary ranges from 2,300 to 3,800 Brazilian reals – the equivalent of 350 to 600 euros – the salary at Oteque, a restaurant that opens from Tuesday to Saturday and only in the evenings, pays fifty per cent above what is offered elsewhere. "We close for two days a week. Opening only for dinner allows us to rest during part of the morning before meeting up to start preparing. Positions, as well as roles, change regularly. For example, there was a young woman who started as a simple waitstaff assistant, but I was impressed by how good she was. Before joining Oteque, she'd worked for a natural products company. However, when I discussed this with her, I discovered that she had a degree in psychology and was fluent in English. I asked her if she'd like to support me more actively on the management side of things. She's now been my personal assistant since early January 2025. When I opened Oteque and moved from São Paulo to Rio, I wanted to – how can I say it – wipe the slate clean, start from scratch. Surround myself only with new people. There was one exception, however: a young guy from Rio who had been the most loyal of the loyal for years at Epice. When I returned to Brazil, he asked if he could come and work with me again. We've been working together for 15 years now. He started working when he was still a child, just 16 years old. He's now reached a good position, and he's getting married soon. Life goes by quickly. It's better to live it well around a shared goal. And together."

When the going gets tough, the tough get going. In order to solve problems, you have to think differently: go against the flow, think outside the box. Great minds come together, meet on equal footing and draw inspiration from one another, and there are many eminent examples of like-minded people who believe in the Think Different approach. An avid reader of biographies, you'll find them all on Alberto Landgraf's bedside table or on the shelves of his library: Einstein, Steve Jobs, Martin Luther King and Michael Jordan. He also quotes from other, less known leaders in particular fields, as well as the most famous. Take Robert Iger, for example, who took risks and surprised people by stepping out of his comfort zone and betting on the future. He saved Walt Disney from an inevitable decline by acquiring Pixar in 2006, Marvel Studios in 2009, Lucasfilm in 2012 and finally 21st Century Fox in 2019. "A true leader, a visionary in his field. Disney's current excellent health is clear proof of that."

Big plans, abrupt changes of direction and potential alterations: these start with the chef himself, who is keen to change his initial approach. A true leader is one who, at the right time, in the right context, knows how to step aside. And they know how to trust their neighbour. Embrace change, encourage the evolution of flavours and share power and responsibility. There is a beginning to everything. Alberto Landgraf has no qualms about admitting that, in the early days of Oteque, the line was more rigid, the chef's role had yet to shed the trappings of power, the demiurgic aura of being the sole guardian of the creative dimension. "I was still testing every aspect of the restaurant – and even the system – that I wanted to create.

The dishes were my responsibility alone, and although I didn't create them in a bubble away from the eyes of others, they were the sheer fruit of my will," he admits, grateful for the generous contributions of others, which he recognises, values and appreciates. "I'm more comfortable with the day-to-day supervision of the Oteque machine now that I've probed its limits and tried to modify certain parts and improve others with a view to achieving a smoother operation. So, it now only seems right and logical to give a small group of trusted colleagues creative autonomy. I'm not giving them carte blanche, but I am sharing with them parameters, ground rules and fields of expression to explore. This is done purely for pragmatic reasons: if we need to work on bitterness, develop other forms of acidity or experiment with textures, they can use their own ideas. They have the tools to do this: the best seasonal produce, as well as all of Oteque's conceptual paraphernalia. I teach them to study on a case-by-case basis and to proceed by blocks, always seeking the perfect equation between balance and maximum expressiveness. They ponder, they try new things, and they let me taste them. Often, they are not of a high enough level. So, I make recommendations and introduce variations and other combinations. We reflect on cooking times and how suitable they are. Like a game of ping pong, this process can go on for quite a while until we jointly acknowledge that a dish is not only good, but also 100 per cent in line with Oteque's ethos. I'm not, strictly speaking, the initiator of that creation, but I participate in its multifaceted vision within the given parameters. Many of the recipes in this chapter, which is specifically devoted to the issue of leadership, have come from the personal insights and reflections of my colleagues," he says, flashing a brief, satisfied smile. Not bad at all for a chef who, in a burst of ironic spontaneity, describes himself as not at all cool. "I swear: cool, in the way it's understood today, just isn't me! I'm, if anything, a boring guy who keeps to himself. At first glance, also not very nice. Not very worldly, I get bored at parties. I don't drink much, just wine – and only the good stuff – and I don't do drugs. In some ways, I'm an old-fashioned guy who believes in hard work and has unwavering values." Let's put it this way: Alberto Landgraf intends to embrace his differences. He knows how the world works, and even more clearly knows that the world of fine dining, with its quirks, routines and approximations and where customers are subjected to a levelling down to the lowest flavour denominator, where everything tastes the same, is not the world he dreams of. Nor did he accept, on the day he decided to make cooking his profession, that it was something irrevocably imposed from above. His vocation is nourished by concrete thoughts and gestures. An undisputed leader who always goes against the status quo and even himself, he knows how long the road ahead of him still is. To become more inclusive and participatory, Oteque must breathe new life into itself every day. Otherwise, he may become an unwilling victim of his own success, suffocating from inertia and laziness. But Alberto Landgraf really is not alone. Eight years of exceptional activity bear witness to the restaurant's uniqueness, showcasing a rare form of true collective solidarity.

**Yogurt ice cream, apple**
→ p. 180

Wagyu, shiitake mushrooms

→ p. 181

**Beetroot tartlet** → p. 182

**Trout roe tartlet** → p. 183

**Truffle tartlet** → p. 184

**Sand perch, endive, vegetable cream**

→ p. 185

Oyster, pimenta de cheiro vinaigrette
→ p. 187

Oyster, Brazil nut milk, caviar
→ p. 188

Oyster, green apple
→ p. 189

Oyster, oyster emulsion
→ p. 190

Oyster, heart of palm
→ p. 191

**Porcini mushrooms, egg yolk**
→ p. 192

Peach sorbet
→ p. 186

Blackberry sorbet, beetroot syrup
→ p. 193

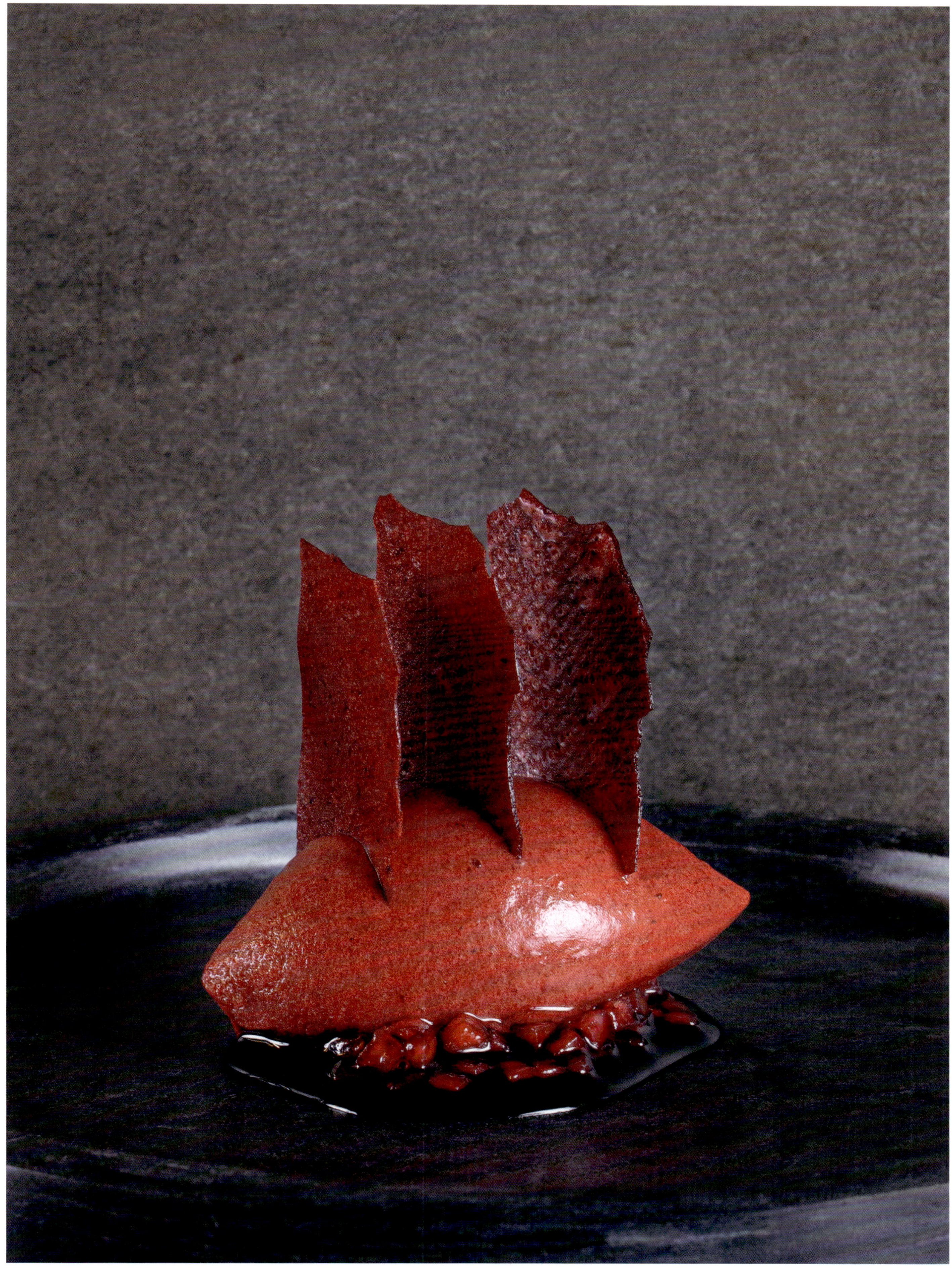

MIND Maps

# YOGURT ICE CREAM, APPLE → p. 162

**For the yogurt ice cream**
- 520g organic Greek yogurt
- 250g whole milk
- 100g sugar
- 55g corn syrup
- 50g skimmed milk powder
- 3.5g dextrose powder
- 2g salt
- 1.5g guar gum
- 0.5g citric acid
- 3 bloomed gold gelatine leaves

**For the caramelized yogurt**
- 500g organic Greek yogurt

**For the yogurt crisp**
- 1kg organic Greek yogurt
- 60g sugar
- 8g xanthan gum
- 2g salt

**For the apple caramel**
- 1kg Fuji apples

**For the apple cubes**
- 1 Fuji apple, peeled and cut into 1cm cubes
- 200g Simple Syrup (page 146)

**For the chervil powder**
- 500g chervil leaves

**Yogurt ice cream**
Put all the ingredients (except the gelatine) in a Thermomix and blend on high speed for 7 minutes, or until it reaches 70°C (158°F). While the mixture is still warm, add the bloomed gelatine leaves and stir or blend to dissolve. Fill a Pacojet beaker with the cream and let it rest in the refrigerator for 24 hours, then freeze at -18°C (0°F). Spin once before serving.

**Caramelized yogurt**
Boil the yogurt in a saucepan for about 1 hour over a low heat until it becomes almost dry. At this point, start stirring it so it doesn't burn – the yogurt protein will caramelize and change the colour of the mixture to light brown. Spread out on a Silpat and dehydrate in a dehydrator at 60°C (140°F) for 24 hours.

**Yogurt crisp**
Put all the ingredients in a Thermomix and blend on high speed until it reaches 70°C (158°F). Pour the mixture into the bowl of a stand mixer and blend until cool. Spread the mixture out on a Silpat in the thinnest layer you can and dehydrate in a dehydrator at 60°C (140°F) for 48 hours. Break into 4 x 6cm pieces.

**Apple caramel**
Juice the apples using a juicer/juice extractor, then strain through a chinois into a saucepan. Boil the apple juice briefly to remove the impurities, then strain through a muslin-lined chinois. Return the juice to the pan and let it reduce until it develops a syrupy consistency.

**Apple cubes**
Combine the cubed apple with the simple syrup in a vacuum bag and seal. Keep in the refrigerator for at least for 2 hours.

**Chervil powder**
Dehydrate the chervil leaves in a dehydrator at 60°C (140°F) for 24 hours, then process in a Thermomix until they form a powder. Sift and reserve in a sealed container.

**Serve**
Put 1 tablespoon of the caramelized yogurt on the plate and shape one scoop of the yogurt ice cream on top. Press the centre of the scoop with a spoon to make a hollow: add the cubed apples in the middle and cover with the apple caramel (enough to fill the hollow). Sprinkle some chervil powder on the yogurt crisps and place a crisp right on top of the ice cream.

—

**Carbon footprint**
whole milk 21.28%; Greek yogurt 21.11%; sugar 16.64%; simple syrup 11.65%; apples 10.79%; chervil leaves 10.43%; skimmed milk powder 4.25%; corn syrup 1.69%; salt 0.78%; xanthan gum 0.68%; gelatine leaves 0.28%; dextrose powder 0.23%; guar gum 0.14%; citric acid 0.05%
**Total emissions per serving**
0.97kg $CO_2e$

# WAGYU, SHIITAKE MUSHROOMS → p. 163

**For the wagyu**
- 750g sirloin A5 wagyu, cut into 6 portions (125g per person), at room temperature
- salt, to taste

**For the shiitake**
- 6 fresh shiitake mushrooms
- generous drizzle of olive oil
- salt, to taste

**To serve**
- Beef Shin Base (page 144), reduced to a thin glaze
- 6 teaspoons Parsley Emulsion (page 147), in a squeezy bottle

**Wagyu**
Preheat the oven to 200°C (392°F). Season each portioned room-temperature wagyu with salt and grill them over hot embers for 40 seconds on each side. Transfer to a baking tray and roast in the oven for 2 minutes. Remove and let them rest, then slice each into 3 equal pieces before serving.

**Shiitake**
Slice each shiitake into 6 equal pieces. Season the mushrooms with the olive oil and salt in a bowl, then grill under a salamander grill at high heat for 2 minutes, or until they caramelize.

**Serve**
Place the wagyu pieces side by side on the plate, then lay the mushrooms on and around them. Finish with 2 tablespoons of the beef base around the wagyu and 1 teaspoon of parsley emulsion in one side of the plate.

—

**Carbon footprint**
A5 wagyu 95.19%; beef shin base 4.19%; olive oil 0.41%; salt 0.11%; parsley emulsion 0.06%; shiitake mushrooms 0.04%
**Total emissions per serving**
14.09kg $CO_2e$

# BEETROOT TARTLET → p. 165

- elderflowers, to serve

**For the tartlet**
- 140g sweet cassava starch (tapioca starch)
- 140g rice flour
- 70g chickpea flour
- 70g almond flour
- 112g coconut oil
- 10g olive oil
- 5g salt
- 140–160g cold water

**For the curd**
- 100g double cream
- 300g whole milk
- 75g white vinegar
- salt, to taste

**For the beetroot**
- 1 large beetroot
- olive oil, for brushing
- salt, to taste

**Tartlet**
Sift all the dry ingredients and put them in the bowl of a stand mixer fitted with the dough hook, add the oils and salt and blend until smooth. Gradually add the water until the dough starts to stick to the sides of the bowl – it should feel slightly dry to the touch, not sticky, and be malleable so you can shape it into a ball (you may not need all the water). Shape 5g of dough per tartlet in a fluted 4cm stainless-steel mould and freeze at -18°C (0°F). Preheat the oven to 155°C (311°F). Bake the tartlet shells covered with another mould (to avoid the dough inflating) for 15–30 minutes until they are light brown and crisp.

**Curd**
Heat the cream and milk in a saucepan until the mixture reaches 80°C (176°F), then turn off the heat, add the vinegar and let the mixture rest for about 1 hour until it curdles and separates. Strain through a muslin-lined chinois to decant. Drain the liquid and discard. Season the curd with salt and place in a piping bag ready to use.

**Beetroot**
Preheat the oven to 150°C (302°F). Put the beetroot in foil, brush it with olive oil and sprinkle with salt, wrap to enclose it in the foil and roast for 2 hours. Let it cool, then peel and cut into small 1cm cubes.

**Serve**
Fill the tartlets with the curd and assemble the beetroot cubes on top. Finish with elderflowers.

—

**Carbon footprint**
milk 45.54%; rice flour 17.72%; coconut oil 13.92%; double cream 6.04%; white vinegar 3.58%; chickpea flour 3.12%; beetroot 2.68%; sweet cassava starch 2.41%; olive oil 2.13%; salt 2.42%; lemon juice 0.35%; water 0.05%; elderflowers 0.04%
**Total emissions per serving**
0.54kg $CO_2e$

# TROUT ROE TARTLET → p. 165

- 6 teaspoons trout roe
- spirulina powder, for sprinkling

**For the tartlet**
- 140g sweet cassava starch (tapioca starch)
- 140g rice flour
- 70g chickpea flour
- 70g almond flour
- 112g coconut oil
- 10g olive oil
- 5g salt
- 140–160g cold water

**For the curd**
- 100g double cream
- 300g whole milk
- 75g white vinegar
- salt, to taste

**Tartlet**
Sift all the dry ingredients and put them in the bowl of a stand mixer fitted with the dough hook, add the oils and salt and blend until smooth. Gradually add the water until the dough starts to stick to the sides of the bowl – it should feel slightly dry to the touch, not sticky, and be malleable so you can shape it into a ball (you may not need all the water). Shape 5g of dough per tartlet in a fluted 4cm stainless-steel mould and freeze at -18°C (0°F). Preheat the oven to 155°C (311°F). Bake the tartlet shells covered with another mould (to avoid the dough inflating) for 15–30 minutes until they are light brown and crisp.

**Curd**
Heat the cream and milk in a saucepan until the mixture reaches 80°C (176°F), then turn off the heat, add the vinegar and let the mixture rest for about 1 hour until it curdles and separates. Strain through a muslin-lined chinois to decant. Drain the liquid and discard. Season the curd with salt and place in a piping bag ready to use.

**Serve**
Fill the tartlets with the curd and cover with 1 teaspoon of the trout roe. Finish with spirulina powder on top.

—

**Carbon footprint**
milk 37.76%; trout roe 20.12%; rice flour 14.68%; coconut oil 11.54%; double cream 5.01%; white vinegar 2.96%; chickpea flour 2.59%; sweet cassava starch 1.99%; olive oil 1.76%; salt 1.44%; spirulina powder 0.08%; water 0.04%; elderflowers 0.03%
**Total emissions per serving**
0.65kg $CO_2e$

# TRUFFLE TARTLET → p. 165

- fresh black truffle, grated, to serve

**For the tartlet**
- 140g sweet cassava starch (tapioca starch)
- 140g rice flour
- 70g chickpea flour
- 70g almond flour
- 112g coconut oil
- 10g olive oil
- 5g salt
- 140–160g cold water

**For the shimeji confit**
- 150g fresh shimeji mushrooms
- 100g olive oil

**For the mashed squash**
- 1 small kabocha squash, halved, deseeded and cut into 4cm-thick slices
- olive oil, for brushing
- salt and black pepper, to taste

**Tartlet**
Sift all the dry ingredients and put them in the bowl of a stand mixer fitted with the dough hook, add the oils and salt and blend until smooth. Gradually add the water until the dough starts to stick to the sides of the bowl – it should feel slightly dry to the touch, not sticky, and be malleable so you can shape it into a ball (you may not need all the water). Shape 5g of dough per tartlet in a fluted 4cm stainless-steel mould and freeze at -18°C (0°F). Preheat the oven to 155°C (311°F). Bake the tartlet shells covered with another mould (to avoid the dough inflating) for 15–30 minutes until they are light brown and crisp.

**Shimeji confit**
Separate the caps from the rest of the mushrooms and place them in a vacuum bag with the olive oil. Steam at 90°C (194°F) for 25 minutes. Let them cool to room temperature and keep in the refrigerator overnight (in the bag) before using.

**Mashed squash**
Preheat the oven to 150°C (302°F). Brush each slice of squash with olive oil and sprinkle with salt, then wrap in foil and roast in the oven for 1 hour 30 minutes. Press the squash pulp through a tamis, season with salt and black pepper to taste, and place in a piping bag.

**Serve**
Fill the tartlets with the mashed squash and assemble ½ teaspoon of the shimeji confit on top. Finish with grated truffle.

—

**Carbon footprint**
olive oil 35.51%; rice flour 23.67%; coconut oil 18.6%; salt 6.95%; chickpea flour 4.17%; truffle 4.08%; sweet cassava starch 3.21%; shimeji mushrooms 3.07%; black pepper 0.59%; kabocha squash 0.09%; water 0.06%
**Total emissions per serving**
0.41kg $CO_2$e

# SAND PERCH, ENDIVE, VEGETABLE CREAM → p. 168

- 6 teaspoons Pimenta Biquinho Oil (page 146), in a squeezy bottle

**For the vegetable cream**
- 180g Vegetable Base (page 145)
- 150g butter
- 1g xanthan gum
- lemon juice, to taste
- salt, to taste

**For the endive**
- 1 endive, thinly sliced, mostly the white part
- olive oil, for drizzling
- squeeze of lemon juice
- salt, to taste

**For the sand perch**
- 100g fine sea salt, plus extra to taste
- 1kg water
- 1 sand perch, cleaned, gutted and filleted (70g fillet per person)
- olive oil, for drizzling

**To serve**
- Malay apple flowers, to garnish
- Fermented Tomato Powder (page 147), for sprinkling

**Vegetable cream**
Bring the vegetable base to the boil in a saucepan with the butter. Off the heat, add the xanthan, then emulsify with a stick blender. Season with salt and lemon juice.

**Endive**
Place the sliced endive in a bowl and season with olive oil, the lemon juice and salt.

**Sand perch**
Preheat the oven to 90°C (194°F). Dissolve the fine salt in the water in a 10cm-deep 1/3 gastro to make a brine. Immerse the fillets in the brine for 8 minutes, then drain the brine. Dry the fillets with a paper towel. drizzle with olive oil, then put into a baking tray and roast in the oven for 5 minutes.

**Finish**
Mix the vegetable cream with the pimenta biquinho oil, not to emulsify just to combine.

**Serve**
Place the sliced endive in the middle of the plate and place the sand perch on one side. Place 2 tablespoons of vegetable cream on the other side, and some Malay apple flowers on the endive. Finish with sprinkled fermented tomato powder on top of the sand perch.

—

**Carbon footprint**
sand perch 43.73%; salt 29.14%; butter 13.03%; olive oil 5.16%; vegetable base 4.94%; endive 2.42%; lemon juice 0.56%; pimenta biquinho oil 0.46%; water 0.27%; xanthan gum 0.13%; fermented tomato powder 0.11%; Malay apple flowers 0.05%
**Total emissions per serving**
0.67kg $CO_2e$

# PEACH SORBET → p. 175

- 3 peaches, cut into 1cm cubes

**For the mashed peaches**
- 1kg peaches
- 50g sugar
- 500g sparkling white wine

**For the crisp peach skin**
- peeled peach skins (above)
- 300g Simple Syrup (page 146)

**For the peach sorbet**
- 750g mashed peaches (above)
- 60g lemon juice
- 60g liquid glucose
- 30g maltodextrin
- 2g citric acid
- 1g salt

**For the white chocolate mousse**
- 180g white chocolate (callets, or bar broken into pieces)
- 300g double cream
- 2 bloomed gold gelatine leaves
- 20g water
- 50g sugar
- 90g egg whites

**For the blackberry powder**
- 500g blackberries

**Mashed peaches**
Blanch the peaches, then peel off their skins (reserve the skins to make the crisp). Halve the peaches, pull away the pits and cook in a pan over a high heat with the sugar and sparkling wine for about 40 minutes, until tender. Strain through a chinois and let them cool in the refrigerator. Blend the peaches in a Thermomix on high speed until smooth. Set aside.

**Crisp peach skin**
Combine the peach skins with the simple syrup in a vacuum bag and seal under full vacuum. Leave for 2 minutes, then strain through a chinois. Dehydrate, without stretching them, in a dehydrator at 60°C (140°F) for 24 hours.

**Peach sorbet**
Put all the ingredients in a Thermomix and blend at high speed for about 10 minutes until smooth. Place in a Pacojet beaker and freeze at -18°C (0°F). Spin once before serving.

**White chocolate mousse**
Melt the white chocolate with 100g of the double cream, then mix with the bloomed gelatine leaves (off the heat) until the gelatine dissolves. Whisk the remaining 200g of cream until soft peaks form (before it turns into Chantilly) and reserve. Boil the measured water and sugar in a saucepan until it reaches 118°C (244.4°F). Whisk the egg whites in the bowl of a stand mixer fitted with the whisk attachment until soft peaks form, then pour the syrup into the bowl, and whisk to make a meringue. Gently stir the white chocolate mixture and start, little by little, incorporating the whipped cream and, finally, the meringue, until everything is homogeneous. Transfer to a siphon with 2 N2O (nitrous oxide) charges and keep it in the refrigerator until ready to serve.

**Blackberry powder**
Blend the blackberries in a Thermomix at high speed for 5 minutes. Strain through a chinois to remove the pulp, spread the seeds out on a Silpat and dehydrate in a dehydrator at 60°C (140°F) for 2 days. Blend in a Thermomix to form a powder. Sift and reserve in a sealed container.

**Serve**
Put the plates in the refrigerator to get cold. Assemble 1 teaspoon of the cubed peaches in the middle of the plate and shape a peach sorbet quenelle on top. Using the siphon, put the white chocolate mousse in a smaller shape beside the sorbet, and fit the dehydrated peach skin on top. Finish with a sprinkle of the blackberry powder.

—

**Carbon footprint**
peaches 30.38%; white chocolate 20.74%; sparkling white wine 14.4%; simple syrup 9.12%; sugar 5.43%; double cream 5.3%; blackberries 5.29%; eggs 3.57%; liquid glucose 2.09%; peach skin 1.53%; maltodextrin 1.46%; lemon juice 0.41%; salt 0.1%; citric acid 0.1%; gelatine leaves 0.1%; water 0.01%
**Total emissions per serving**
1.81kg $CO_2e$

# OYSTER, PIMENTA DE CHEIRO VINAIGRETTE → p. 173

- 6 teaspoons Pimenta de Cheiro Vinaigrette (page 146)
- 3 teaspoons Parsley Oil (page 146)
- coarse salt, to serve

**For the oysters**
- 6 oysters

**For the seaweed vinaigrette**
- 200g Vegetable Base (page 145)
- lemon juice, to taste
- 50g Kombu Oil (page 146)
- salt, to taste
- chives, finely chopped, to taste

**Oysters**
Preheat a steam oven (100% steam) to 180°C (356°F). Clean the oysters to remove any debris, place them whole (with the shells) in the steam oven and cook for 2 minutes to firm them up. Carefully open the oyster shells with an oyster knife, remove the top shell and release the oyster from the muscle on its lower shell, reserving the shell. Set aside at room temperature on a paper towel to drain the liquids until ready to serve.

**Seaweed vinaigrette**
Simmer the vegetable base in a saucepan until it has reduced by half, then remove from the heat and let it cool at room temperature. Season to taste with lemon juice, kombu oil, salt and chives.

**Finish**
Strain the pimenta de cheiro vinaigrette and mix it with the parsley oil.

**Serve**
Put 2 tablespoons of coarse salt at the bottom of the plate, then assemble the oyster, in its lower shell, on top. Cover the oyster with the seaweed vinaigrette and finish with 1 teaspoon of the pimenta de cheiro vinaigrette mixture.

—

**Carbon footprint**
kombu oil 44.4%; oysters 21.52%; vegetable base 15.67%; parsley oil 9.82%; pimenta de cheiro vinaigrette 5.75%; lemon juice 1.61%; salt 0.8%; chives 0.43%
**Total emissions per serving**
0.23kg $CO_2$e

# OYSTER, BRAZIL NUT MILK, CAVIAR → p. 173

**For the oysters**

- 6 oysters

**To serve**

- 6 tablespoons Brazil Nut Milk (page 144)
- chives, thinly sliced
- 6 teaspoons caviar, the best you can get
- Sea Urchin Bottarga (page 147), grated
- coarse salt

**Oysters**

Preheat a steam oven (100% steam) to 180°C (356°F). Clean the oysters to remove any debris, place them whole (with the shells) in the steam oven and cook for 2 minutes to firm them up. Carefully open the oyster shells with an oyster knife, remove the top shell and release the oyster from the muscle on its lower shell, reserving the shell. Set aside at room temperature on a paper towel to drain the liquids until ready to serve.

**Serve**

Put 2 tablespoons of coarse salt at the bottom of the plate, then assemble the oyster, in its lower shell, on top. Cover the oyster with 1 tablespoon of Brazil nut milk, a pinch of chives and finish with 1 teaspoon of caviar and about 0.2g grated sea urchin.

—

**Carbon footprint**

caviar 41.68%; Brazil nut milk 29.56%; oysters 28.3%; sea urchin bottarga 0.29%; chives 0.17%

**Total emissions per serving**

0.18kg $CO_2e$

# OYSTER, GREEN APPLE → p. 173

**For the oysters**

- 6 oysters

**For the green apple juice**

- 400g green apple juice, extracted in a juicer
- 30g parsley, leaves picked
- 50g chervil, leaves picked
- 100g rapeseed oil
- 1g xanthan gum
- juice of 1 lemon

**For the pickled green apple**

- 1 green apple, cut into 2mm cubes, unpeeled
- 100g Simple Syrup (page 146)
- 100g white vinegar

**To serve**

- Parsley Oil (page 146), in a squeezy bottle
- coarse salt

**Oysters**

Preheat a steam oven (100% steam) to 180°C (356°F). Clean the oysters to remove any debris, place them whole (with the shells) in the steam oven and cook for 2 minutes to firm them up. Carefully open the oyster shells with an oyster knife, remove the top shell and release the oyster from the muscle on its lower shell, reserving the shell. Set aside at room temperature on a paper towel to drain the liquids until ready to serve.

**Green apple juice**

Pour the green apple juice into a saucepan and bring to the boil until it forms a foam. Remove from the heat and strain through muslin, then cool in the refrigerator. Combine the parsley and chervil leaves and the green apple juice in a Thermomix and blend for 3 minutes at high speed. Strain through a chinois, then emulsify the mixture with a stick blender, gradually adding the rapeseed oil. Finally, blend in the xanthan briefly and season with the lemon juice.

**Pickled green apple**

Combine the cubed apples with the simple syrup and vinegar in a vacuum bag and seal under full vacuum.

**Serve**

Place 2 tablespoons of coarse salt at the bottom of the plate, then assemble the oyster, in its lower shell, on top. Cover the oyster with the green apple juice and finish with ½ teaspoon of pickled green apple and drops of parsley oil around.

—

**Carbon footprint**

rapeseed oil 23.15%; simple syrup 18.33%; oysters 16.43%; green apple juice 13.59%; white vinegar 8.41%; parsley oil 7.5%; green apple 5.09%; lemon juice 2.87%; parsley 2.37%; chervil leaves 1.97%; xanthan gum 0.29%

**Total emissions per serving**

0.31kg $CO_2e$

# OYSTER, OYSTER EMULSION → p. 173

**For the oysters**
- 6 oysters

**For the oyster emulsion**
- 15 oysters
- 2 bunches of parsley, leaves picked
- 100g rapeseed oil
- 1g xanthan gum
- squeeze of lemon juice
- salt, to taste

**To serve**
- 10g finger lime
- 12 mizuna leaves or Japanese mustard greens
- coarse salt

**Oysters**
Preheat a steam oven (100% steam) to 180°C (356°F). Clean the oysters to remove any debris, place them whole (with the shells) in the steam oven and cook for 2 minutes to firm them up. Carefully open the oyster shells with an oyster knife, remove the top shell and release the oyster from the muscle on its lower shell, reserving the shell. Set aside at room temperature on a paper towel to drain the liquids until ready to serve.

**Oyster emulsion**
Preheat a steam oven (100% steam) to 180°C (356°F). Rinse the oysters and place them whole on a tray, with the shells intact, in the steam oven for 4 minutes. Carefully open the oyster shells with an oyster knife, remove the top shell and release the oyster from the muscle on its lower shell. Cool the oysters in the refrigerator, then transfer them to a Thermomix with the parsley leaves and blend for 2 minutes at high speed. Strain through a tamis, then gradually add the rapeseed oil, emulsifying the mixture with a stick blender until soft. Add the xanthan and stir just to incorporate. Season with salt and the lemon juice.

**Serve**
Place 2 tablespoons of coarse salt at the bottom of the plate, then assemble the oyster, in its lower shell, on top. Cover the oyster with the oyster emulsion and finish with finger lime vesicles and 2 mizuna leaves.

—

**Carbon footprint**
oysters 62%; rapeseed oil 24.96%; parsley 5.11%; salt 4.61%; finger lime 2.08%; lemon juice 0.88%; xanthan gum 0.32%; mizuna leaves 0.04%
**Total emissions per serving**
0.29kg $CO_2$e

# OYSTER, HEART OF PALM → p. 173

**For the oysters**
- 6 oysters

**For the heart of palm juice**
- 1.5kg fresh heart of palm, cut into 5mm cubes
- 100g rapeseed oil
- 1g xanthan gum
- lemon juice, to taste

**For the cooked heart of palm**
- 200g fresh heart of palm
- generous amount of olive oil
- 2g salt

**To serve**
- Pimenta Biquinho Oil (page 146), in a squeezy bottle
- 6g Shio Kombu Particles (page 147), finely chopped
- picked chervil leaves
- coarse salt

**Oysters**
Preheat a steam oven (100% steam) to 180°C (356°F). Clean the oysters to remove any debris, place them whole (with the shells) in the steam oven and cook for 2 minutes to firm them up. Carefully open the oyster shells with an oyster knife, remove the top shell and release the oyster from the muscle on its lower shell, reserving the shell. Set aside at room temperature on a paper towel to drain the liquids until ready to serve.

**Heart of palm juice**
Sear the palm heart cubes in a frying pan over a high heat, until toasted on all sides, then blend them in a juicer while still hot. Strain through a muslin-lined chinois into a saucepan and boil the juice until foam forms. Strain again through a muslin-lined chinois and cool in the refrigerator. Gradually add the rapeseed oil, using a stick blender to emulsify the mixture, then finally incorporate the xanthan. Season with lemon juice.

**Cooked heart of palm**
Preheat a steam oven (100% steam) to 100°C (212°F). Combine the whole heart of palm, a generous drizzle of olive oil and the salt in a vacuum bag, seal under full vacuum and cook in the steam oven for 50 minutes. Drain and cut into small 2mm dice.

**Serve**
Put 2 tablespoons of coarse salt at the bottom of the plate, then assemble the oyster, in its lower shell, on top. Cover the oyster with the heart of palm juice and ½ teaspoon of the cooked and diced heart of palm. Finish with drops of pimenta biquinho oil, a sprinkle of the shio kombu particles and the chervil.

—

**Carbon footprint**
heart of palm 90.42%; rapeseed oil 4.55%; oysters 3.23%; shio kombu 1.11%; olive oil 1.14%; pimenta biquinho oil 0.3%; lemon juice 0.12%; chervil leaves 0.06%; xanthan gum 0.06%
**Total emissions per serving**
1.58kg $CO_2e$

# PORCINI MUSHROOMS, EGG YOLK → p. 174

**For the porcini**

- 6 fresh porcini mushrooms
- drizzle of olive oil
- 80g butter, cubed
- salt, to taste

**For the mushroom broth**

- drizzle of olive oil
- 200g fresh shiitake mushrooms, roughly chopped
- 200g fresh porcini mushrooms, roughly chopped
- 200g button mushrooms, roughly chopped
- 2 shallots, roughly chopped
- 20g thyme, whole sprigs
- 50g dried shiitake mushrooms
- 50g dried mushrooms
- 50g dried porcini mushrooms
- 20g kombu
- 5kg water

**For the egg yolk emulsion**

- 6 free range or organic eggs
- 60g mushroom broth (above)
- 8g sugar cane vinegar
- salt, to taste

**To serve**

- fresh porcini mushrooms
- white, yellow and purple Egyptian star cluster flowers
- 6 teaspoons Mushroom Vinaigrette (page 145)

**Porcini**

Gently clean the mushrooms with a wet towel to remove all the dirt, then gently peel the stalk. Cut the mushrooms in half from top to bottom and mark a crosshatch on both inside (cut) surfaces. Heat a cast-iron pan over a high heat, add the olive oil and the cubed butter and then the porcini, cut side down, and sauté until caramelized. Remove from the pan and season to taste with salt.

**Mushroom broth**

Heat the olive oil in a large stock pot over a high heat, add the mushrooms and sauté for 6 minutes, or until caramelized. Add the shallots, thyme and the dry ingredients and cover with the water. Simmer for 1 hour, then strain the broth through a chinois into a clean pan and reduce by half.

**Egg yolk emulsion**

Cook the eggs in a thermocirculator at 63°C (145.4°F) for 1 hour, then transfer the eggs to an ice bath. Carefully crack the eggs open and separate the yolks from the whites (you are using only the yolks). Whisk the yolks and the warm mushroom broth together in a bowl and season with the vinegar and some salt.

**Serve**

Put a spoon of the finished egg yolk emulsion in the centre of the plate, put 2 warm grilled porcini pieces around it, then slice fresh porcinis on a mandoline and lay them and the flowers on the plate as garnish. Finish with 1 teaspoon of mushroom vinaigrette on top of the egg yolk.

—

**Carbon footprint**

eggs 27.02%; dried shiitake mushrooms 22.61%; dried porcini mushrooms 11.35%; kombu 9.18%; butter 7.13%; fresh porcini mushrooms 7.12%; olive oil 4.25%; fresh shiitake mushrooms 2.04%; button mushrooms 2.04%; salt 1.39%; water 1.09%; shallots 0.53%; sugar cane vinegar 0.42%; thyme 0.29%; Egyptian star cluster flowers 0.05%

**Total emissions per serving**

0.82kg $CO_2$e

# BLACKBERRY SORBET, BEETROOT SYRUP → p. 177

- 5 strawberries, cut into 2mm cubes

**For the glucose syrup**
- 1.5kg water
- 300g sugar
- 450g liquid glucose

**For the blackberry sorbet**
- 500g blackberries
- 300g glucose syrup (above)
- 100g Simple Syrup (page 146)
- 30g lemon juice
- 3g ice cream stabilizer

**For the beetroot syrup**
- 5kg beetroots

**For the dried blackberries**
- 500g blackberries
- 35g sweet cassava starch (tapioca starch)
- 50g sugar

**Glucose syrup**
Combine the water, sugar and glucose in a saucepan and cook until it boils and the sugar has dissolved. Transfer to the refrigerator to cool down. Reserve.

**Blackberry sorbet**
Blend the blackberries in a Thermomix at high speed for 10 minutes or until they reach a homogeneous texture, then strain through a chinois. Combine the berry pulp with the glucose syrup, simple syrup, lemon juice and the ice cream stabilizer in a bowl and place in a Pacojet beaker. Freeze at -18°C (0°F).

**Beetroot syrup**
Blend the beetroots (skin on) in a Thermomix at high speed for 8 minutes until they reach a homogeneous texture, then transfer the pulp to a saucepan and bring to the boil until a foam forms on the surface. Strain through a muslin-lined chinois into a clean pan, then reduce over a low heat until it turns into a sticky syrup. Put the syrup in a squeezy bottle.

**Dried blackberries**
Blend the blackberries in a Thermomix at high speed for 10 minutes until creamy in consistency, then strain through a chinois. Dilute the sweet cassava starch with a little water, then combine this with the berry pulp and sugar. Transfer to a saucepan and cook over a low heat, stirring, until the mixture thickens. Spread it out on a Silpat and dehydrate in a dehydrator at 60°C (140°F) for 24 hours. Break into 4 x 6cm pieces.

**Serve**
Put 1 teaspoon of the fresh cubed strawberries on a plate, then lay ⅓ teaspoon of the beetroot syrup on top. Arrange a scoop of the blackberry sorbet on top and finish with 3 pieces of the dry blackberries.

—

**Carbon footprint**
beetroots 43.01%; liquid glucose 19.93%; blackberries 15.62%; sugar 13.32%; strawberries 5.41%; simple syrup 1.9%; tapioca starch 0.26%; ice cream stabilizer 0.18%; water 0.18%; lemon juice 0.15%; pollen 0.04%
**Total emissions per serving**
1.48kg $CO_2$e

05

# CREATIVE PROCESS

Upon his death, the English poet Stephen Spender (1909–1995), a close friend of Christopher Isherwood and Wystan Hugh (W. H.) Auden, left humanity a varied oeuvre. This included not only poems, but also a beautiful autobiographical novel (*The Temple*, Faber & Faber, 1988) about life in inter-war Weimar Berlin, which was worlds away from the constraints of the somewhat still chastity-belted Victorian-like society, as well as a treasure trove of reflections on art and society, which he diligently recorded in his diary from 1939 to 1983 (*Journals*, Faber & Faber, 1985). Considered to be his absolute masterpiece, *World Within World* (Hamish Hamilton, 1951) is more circumscribed, falling somewhere between literary criticism and introspection, and almost foreshadowing the genre of today's autofiction. On page 300 of the 1951 edition, Spender writes: "Fiction and clinically analytic writing extend our knowledge of human personality, but they also offer avenues of escape from the glaring light of consciousness of him who says: 'I am I'." The following paragraph continues: "It is in the individual who accepts the responsibility of his own complexity, that the diversity of society attains a unity of consciousness where opposites are reconciled."

Not one for storytelling, Alberto Landgraf is wary of autobiographical fiction. If anything, he invents dynamic references for each project to keep the creative act at a good distance from his id. This is at odds with much of the cuisine in vogue these days, in which a chef's identity is central. This idea can, incidentally, be transferred to other fields, such as film and literature, in which, like signature cuisine, there is an implicit, authoritarian reference to a single demiurgic and causal figure.

Landgraf is wary of self-aggrandising power and bombastic speeches. He has far too many other interests to occupy himself with. In fact, when he talks about himself, his motivations and his aspirations, he often gets sidetracked. Speaking of which: "My brother worked as an agronomist for years on an important organic plantation in the Paraty region, in the heart of the Costa Verde, surrounded by the Atlantic Forest, which is now a UNESCO World Heritage Site. Paraty was famous from the 15th century onwards for its ancient fishing port, from where Portuguese ships would set sail for Lisbon after raiding our stores of fresh foodstuffs. Like my brother, I feel a strong connection to this region. However, we took different paths. When he was a teenager, he dreamed of becoming a heavy metal musician. As a fledgling guitarist, he knew he had to practise if he wanted to improve and become the best in his field. This meant studying music and exploring all styles and forms, from punk and classical to bossa nova and blues. At the end of this journey, he tried to find his own path. But for a cook, I learnt that, in the heat of the moment, very different dynamics come into play."

So, should you learn the art and then cast it aside? Not necessarily. Landgraf took the traditional route of an apprenticeship, familiarising himself with basic culinary techniques, which were, of course in those days, French. However, as Gertrude Stein said, "a rose is a rose is a rose", so too a dumpling is a dumpling is a dumpling. Just as a soufflé ultimately remains a soufflé. There are not a thousand ways to make it; if you aim for perfection, you have to adapt to a tried-and-tested tradition and this allows for *only* limited variations. However, when intuition suggests another way, offering an escape from routine and the daily repetition of immutable tasks, the path of creation does not follow the beaten track. Instead, it reveals itself to be a crossroads leading to unexpected life experiences. A eureka moment cannot be grasped simply through sheer willpower. If anything, it lies in the miracle of being in the right place at the right time when a glimmer of possibility surfaces. Or it falls on you unexpectedly – to borrow an expression dear to this former applied physics student – like the apple that fell on Isaac Newton's head while sitting under that famous tree.

For Albert Landgraf, his "bump on the head" was the unexpected outcome of what, at first, his parents could – and should – have taken as a mere gap year. "I studied physics, and I was good at it, too, but I was bored. I wanted a change," he says, remembering those days when he wanted to get everything done quickly. "One day, I saw a programme about backpacking on television. I think it was on the Discovery Channel or CNN. And I had a kind of teenage epiphany. I don't know how, but I managed to convince my parents – who were obviously very reluctant at first – to let me spend a year travelling around Europe, then stay in London with an old family friend who worked in finance. I justified

it as an educational experience: doesn't travelling shape you when you're young? I got the go-ahead. And as clear rules make for lasting relationships, we agreed that, after a year, I would return home to work. And, always in the eyes of my parents, mend my ways like a well-behaved prodigal son. My European explorations began in Basel, with obvious stops in Paris, where I visited the Louvre – a dream come true! I'd recently arrived in London and, as is often the case, had already blown all the money I'd been given for my stay. To support myself and pay for language courses to improve my English, I found a job in a bar-restaurant called, and I swear I'm not making this up: Cappuccino. Things were going quite well for me, and I caught the eye of chef Neville Campbell, who took me under his wing. One day – since I was always willing and never said no to anything – he asked me if I'd be interested in working in the kitchen of Anouska Hempel's Blakes, one of London's first boutique hotels in the residential neighbourhood of South Kensington. They were looking for someone to handle not only breakfasts, but also the four dishes offered on their short menu. The only thing left to do was muster the courage to tell my father over the phone that I wouldn't be honouring our agreement. I was afraid of their reaction as my parents definitely weren't expecting it. My dad in particular. But with the help of their old friend, who supported me, I managed to convince them to come round to my way of seeing things."

If you rummage through the family archives, there should still be some vintage photos of the young, former future Brazilian physicist, supposedly under the auspices of Einstein and Newton, flirting instead with the all black Gothic-baroque imaginarium of Anouska Hempel's hotel. Good for him: the interior designer, muse of her almost private *maison d'hôtes* for evening-gown clad creatures out of a Tim Burton film starring Helena Bonham Carter, had an eye for young talent. And as she was also the celebrated interior decorator of Tom Aikens' brand new restaurant, if he felt ready for such a big leap, assuming he wasn't afraid to work long and hard, there was definitely a spot for him. "So, I found myself in the right place at the right time, at Tom's. I then went on to Gordon Ramsay's for a baptism of fire at the very heart of fine dining at the highest level. However, I quickly found the strict rules and total self-denial it demanded to be too dehumanising, with no possibility of rehumanisation. It seemed unbalanced to me. Even back then, I felt that a balance between work, life and personal interests was the cornerstone of my quest. Work better, and in a more reasoned way."

Some people are silent; some gesticulate to make themselves understood. There are those who expatiate on their many motivations and fanciful intentions. And there are those who, like Landgraf, put pen and paper to declare their affection for the geometric shape of a triangle. It hardly matters that he has forgotten the exact term: "It's the one with the three 60-degree sides, the same size as the inner one. It's the figure that roughly, at least, sums up my aspiration for that balance between research, daily restaurant work and personal life."

More specifically, it represents the three cardinal points of his creative atlas: texture, acidity and temperature. Three poles around which his sense of direction revolves. He never works on autopilot; instead, he applies the physics lessons he learnt during his university days, juggling on the stove exercises that are indirectly connected. Theory willingly yields to empirical research: "I always start with my surroundings, with ingredients, and consider a possible dialogue. I measure the extent of the affinity among them. A bit like an architect adding or subtracting elements to achieve the desired balance. It's like a reference table: what goes with what? In the world of Western cooking, when constructing a menu, you proceed dish by dish and categorise the ingredients. There must be proteins, vegetables and perhaps carbohydrates. For example, you could combine chicken with a purée, spinach and a tomato salad. Let's take three ingredients as examples, three identities in their own right: besides chicken, let's focus on apples and also vanilla. I can make a vanilla ice cream. But vanilla also goes well with tofu, so why not try making a vanilla tofu cream with the potatoes? Which, by the way, would go very well with the chicken. Maybe with roasted apples. That is where the field of possibilities opens up. Do we want something sweet or savoury? If we're developing a new dessert, we could start with the idea of a tofu and apple ice cream. And why not try a tofu and potato ice cream? It could be developed into a tofu, vanilla and potato ice cream, which, ideally, would be served with caramelised apples. In cooking, we isolate every element, trying to study every variation imaginable. But beware of the dizzying array of possibilities! Which type of apple best suits what we want to achieve? Each variety has its own unique properties and taste qualities. Fujis are sugary and crisp, which makes them very different from the much tarter Granny Smiths. I then have to balance the latter with honey or perhaps even sugar. When cooked, they are ideal for desserts and are best served hot rather than cold. I'll then increase the temperature until I'm happy with the consistency, ensuring that they are still slightly crispy on the outside and creamy inside – chewability is important. Yes, it's creamy but just right. We have to be extremely careful, though, because if we push the creaminess too far, we risk ending up with... baby food! All this circumstantial research is multiplied ad infinitum, ingredient by ingredient, variation by variation, enabling us to adapt to almost any situation. I share pages and pages of notes, feedback, sketches and diagrams with my colleagues. In a nutshell, my creative process is based on a reference table that is applied to situations and ingredients on a case-by-case basis. This allows me to avoid the pitfalls of creating a menu from scratch and according to rigid timeframes. Instead, it gives me the freedom to create in a far more responsive way. I can adapt dishes, ingredients and techniques on the spur of the moment or according to my own or my customers' wishes."

Oteque is, in every respect, a singular restaurant. A pragmatic think tank. With its own practices, instructions for use and scope for experimentation. A unique example of today's culinary landscape, not only in Latin America, yet at the same time it is also not an ivory tower. Not because Landgraf rarely displays all-embracing, maximal philosophical systems, or that he's boastful or part of the establishment. A lone ranger, a free electron, Alberto Landgraf lays claims to it under everyone's gaze. With an obvious urge to share, with a desire to break down unnecessary barriers. Raising the level of the discussion. Training here is never rushed; there's always just enough time to quickly adapt to the current house rules on cooking. The focus is on the long-term process, not how long it actually takes. Landgraf nurtures a young and dynamic team, making them as autonomous as possible through progressive growth based on the free flow of knowledge. No arrogance here. "I prefer to choose young collaborators with little experience of working in other restaurants of the same level, and I tend to favour those with an almost blank CV, so as not to find myself surrounded by well-trained chefs and assistants who are therefore inevitably predictable. When I talk about balance, a functional system and a mindset to streamline the various constraints of creative restaurant management, it is not only in my immediate interest. It is also to help the rest of the team understand that focusing on balance, on a methodology of indirect association can lead to a more practical, more hygienic and humane restaurant management. And that's the real goal."

Let's now imagine an empty theatre. Alberto Landgraf is under house arrest like everyone else, pacing up and down, forced into idleness like the rest of the world, taken by surprise by the pandemic. To break the monotony, one fine morning at the height of COVID, he decides to shoot a video to post online, a sign of life driven by the pure spirit of pedagogy. He admits in hindsight that it was pretty ugly, a rough and ready production with a camera on a tripod set up for a long take. In it, Landgraf is in the centre, showing sketches and drawing diagrams, in full flow as he explains his idea that blocks are the key to creative construction. This amateur, homemade video, downloadable for just a few dollars, is a message in a bottle tossed into the sea for youngsters and any restaurant professionals who are interested. In it, he displays not so much his radical diversity, but presents an approach to creation and resources – including human resources – that could be useful for many other people. Thinking outside the box and away from the conventional orthodoxy of the culinary world, this Brazilian chef was thinking out loud about applied altruism, but never expected such mixed reactions. "There were even some violent ones," he recalls, still amazed a few years later. Questioning old habits and rigid hierarchies, trampling on the hornet's nest of fossilised habits.

Allow us to hazard a guess, with the added bonus of a hunch. Perhaps that video that caused such a stir was missing something: a live transcript of life. A vessel for communication. Let there be a digression and an example. Let's take the concept of temperature. One thing is the methodological in vitro analysis within a restaurant, shared by those at the stove in a plenary session. Verbalising a thought and a personal epiphany is quite another matter. Alberto Landgraf himself acknowledges this when he reflects on the vast gulf between the standard practice of gastronomic restaurants – "from the stove to the pass, with the sole aim of ensuring the dish is always served hot to customers" – and his own experience. With a mischievous smile, he recalls his second trip to Japan several years ago. He'd gone to a renowned, very niche sushi restaurant just outside Tokyo, about twenty minutes from the district of Ginza, getting there at noon on the dot for when it opened. "But something wasn't quite right. Strangely, we were made to queue outside, waiting for them to let us in: hardly the famous Japanese art of hospitality. The cook finally opened the door and came out. He apologised for the inconvenience and asked if we could kindly wait a little longer. Five minutes or so. Of course, no problem. I'd moved heaven and earth to get this reservation; I was hardly going to budge now. Five minutes turned into ten. But once inside, I tried to understand why, in a country where precision and punctuality are golden rules, we had been made to wait outside. At first, I couldn't believe it. Apparently, the freshly cooked sushi rice was too hot to be served; it needed to cool down first. Everything needs its own time – it was better to wait until the rice was at the right temperature than to serve it at the wrong one. Each element must be perfect in its own right. In that restaurant, where traditionally all the diners were served at the same time, they chose to make an exception to the rule; rather than compromising on quality by serving rice that was not at the right temperature, they made us wait. This would be unimaginable anywhere else in the world. However, achieving the perfect temperature was absolutely essential for fully appreciating the different nuances of the sushi."

It would be lovely, a dream shared by all, to clear away the dregs of language and invent a new, personal grammar built on experience. But what if, for Alberto Landgraf – someone who could hardly pass for an ascetic – that dream rested fully on the experience of emptiness? To explain himself, he cites the significant influence of a short book, some eighty pages long, which he read on a shinkansen, travelling at high speed from the bustling metropolis of Tokyo to the imperial city of Kyoto, famed for its thousand temples. "In *White*, a slim volume whose small size is inversely proportional to the depth of its musings, Kenya Hara – one of the most distinguished designers of his generation, who was, among other things, the art director of Muji for years before recently heading the Science of Design department at Musashino Art University – talks about the experience of emptiness. In very simple but profound theoretical language, it states that if we build a house, for example, the moment we conceive and construct it, it exists, factually, it is a concrete reality. Albeit temporary, because it is built in a void. In nothingness, our conception of the house is merely a space granted to us, borrowed momentarily from the experience of emptiness. Which, on the contrary, is permanent, while everything else, whatever we do or plan, remains ephemeral. Built precisely on emptiness." A surprising revelation requiring slow, introspective processing. A personal process of developing concepts and related manual practices that has led this

Brazilian chef to share the same meticulous reflection on the essentiality of gesture in time and space with Kenya Hara. Almost a motto: "Simplify the sophisticated, sophisticate what is too simple." It is the guiding line that underpins the daily activities of the entire Oteque team. A gradual transition from the deus ex machina towards collective practices and the serene compulsion of a happy conclusion. Subtracting the innate values of merit to highlight the unique qualities of each ingredient – just like the triangle mentioned in a previous chapter, of which the base is equivalent to the two lateral angles. Cost becomes nonsense, and even humble ingredients find their rightful place. Even broccoli, which has been a victim of culinary abuse for centuries – boiled and overcooked to within an inch of its life – has a refined and noble place at Oteque. Transformed from a mere side dish into the mainstay on the plate. Cooked for up to four hours over a low heat throughout the afternoon before the evening service, it retains all of its texture and intensity of flavour. Landgraf sometimes likes to use coconut milk, a plant-based fat that is not only the preserve of vegans, to temper its bitterness. However, when taken in isolation, even cacao can be categorised as a fat and used accordingly with certain foods. In contrast, pork fat is far superior to olive oil: "Even the best olive oil can develop a metallic aftertaste at high temperatures, which I dislike because it unbalances an ingredient." It is ideal for cooking octopus and squid over an open flame, which emphasises the animalistic nature of this intentional surf-and-turf dish.

Chef Landgraf has something of an entomologist's soul: unlike most people, he loves to classify, write, draw, cut out, compose and annotate his illustrated fact sheets, which are arranged by product families and possible affinities. He then moves on to the hands-on side of things with his assistants, applying empirical criteria of both addition and subtraction. "Not everything goes with everything. Even when we eliminate approximations and incompatibilities, I feel that every choice is like an empty page that we can fill at that precise moment with our intuition and new possibilities can be found." In moments of success, as well as during periods of ongoing research, Alberto Landgraf certainly wonders how much he owes to his analytical spirit, which has always informed his work as a creative cook. You most likely won't find it on his CV or among the highlights of his culinary successes, but as he himself hints, there's a large dose of it somewhere. "I'm good with numbers. I move with a certain agility on a conceptual level. I never completed my physics degree as I did only three years instead of the required four. Perhaps it was because, unconsciously – and I say this now with the benefit of hindsight, as someone who questions everything relative, that I was far too dazzled by the figure of Einstein – it wasn't the right discipline for me. Nowadays, physics is regarded as an exact science in the same way as mathematics, but in my opinion it's closer to philosophy. Perhaps I should have become a mathematician. In physics, you can make inferences and assumptions, but you always remain in the abstract.

Ultimately, to avoid barking up the wrong tree and to ensure you're on the right track, you must always ask a mathematician to verify your calculations. Personally, and theoretically, I can accept the idea of living without knowing, but as a cook, in order to move forward and improve, to explore new paths, I need the right answer to every nagging question, doubt or problem. And, what's more, the most exact one there is." With every sitting, Oteque is proof that cooking – at least in Alberto Landgraf's case – can be as analytical as an exact science. Without forgetting the creative effervescence he is known for. But he also has a trump card: the continual pursuit of a logical conversation between the ethics of taste and the natural pleasure of sharing with others. Without that wavering yet essential balance, the Oteque equation would never have come to fruition. But the history of contemporary cuisine decided otherwise.

Snapper, kale, heart of palm, pumpkin seed

→ p. 237

**Sea urchin, onion, mussel cream**
→ p. 231

**Brioche, sardine, foie gras**
→ p. 235

**Scallop, fish mayonnaise**
→ p. 232

**Cashew cream, coconut foam, trout roe**
→ p. 234

Duck heart, beetroot cream

→ p. 233

Açaí sorbet, rapadura crumbs
→ p. 238

**Brazil nut ice cream**
→ p. 236

**Sweetcorn ice cream**
→ p. 230

# SWEETCORN ICE CREAM → p. 227

- wood sorrel leaves, to garnish

**For the sweetcorn ice cream**
- 30g butter
- 600g fresh sweetcorn kernels, stripped from the cob
- pinch of salt
- 80g sugar
- 600g whole milk
- 20g skimmed milk powder
- 200g double cream, chilled

**For the chocolate and fondant crisps**
- 1.2kg fondant blanc
- 800g liquid glucose
- 800g chocolate, 30% cocoa solids

**For the rapadura crumbs**
- 100g rapadura
- 100g ground almonds
- 100g black Dutch-processed cocoa powder

**Sweetcorn ice cream**
Melt the butter in a frying pan over a high heat, add the corn and pinch of salt and sauté for 10 minutes, until caramelized. Blend the sautéed corn at room temperature in a Thermomix with the sugar, whole milk and skimmed milk powder at high speed for 8 minutes or until smooth, then pour it into a bowl and stir gently with the chilled cream. Pour into a Pacojet beaker and freeze at -18°C (0°F). Spin once before serving.

**Chocolate and fondant crisps**
Combine all the ingredients in a saucepan and bring to the boil over a low heat. Spread out quickly on a Silpat and let it cool to room temperature, then break into 4 x 6cm pieces.

**Rapadura crumbs**
Preheat the oven to 100°C (212°F). Finely grate the rapadura, mix it with the ground almonds and cocoa powder and roast in a shallow gastropan for 1 hour. Let the mixture cool to room temperature, then blend in the Thermomix at high speed until crumbs form.

**Serve**
Place 1 teaspoon of the rapadura crumbs in the middle of a deep plate and a scoop of the sweetcorn ice cream on top. Finish with 2 chocolate and fondant crisps, lined up on the top of the ice cream. Garnish the ice cream with wood sorrel leaves.

—

**Carbon footprint**
chocolate 38.71%; fondant 22.38%; liquid glucose 10.72%; whole milk 10.2%; black cocoa powder 6.47%; sweetcorn 5.34%; rapadura 1.82%; sugar 1.66%; double cream 1.35%; ground almonds 0.72%; butter 0.36%; skimmed milk powder 0.24%; salt 0.02%; wood sorrel leaves 0.01%
**Total emissions per serving**
4.85kg $CO_2e$

# SEA URCHIN, ONION, MUSSEL CREAM → p. 212

- 180g sea urchin
- lemon juice, to taste
- salt, to taste
- oregano leaves, to garnish

**For the corn farofa**
- 40g butter
- 150g corn farofa
- 1.5g salt

**For the roasted onions**
- 2 onions

**For the mussel cream**
- olive oil, for drizzling
- 500g unshelled mussels, scrubbed and debearded
- 1 onion, finely chopped
- 1 leek, trimmed, rinsed and finely chopped
- a few thyme sprigs, to taste
- 200g white wine
- 20g dried shiitake mushrooms
- 20g kombu
- 1kg double cream
- squeeze of lemon juice
- salt, to taste

**Corn farofa**
Melt the butter over a high heat in a frying pan, add the farofa and salt and toast for 5 minutes.

**Roasted onions**
Preheat the oven to 180ºC (356ºF). Wrap the onions in foil and roast in the oven for 2 hours. Leave the onions to cool, halve them lengthways and separate the onion layers.

**Mussel cream**
Heat a drizzle of olive oil in a large saucepan over a high heat and sauté the mussels. Add the onion, leek and thyme sprigs to the pan and sweat for 5 minutes, then deglaze the pan with the white wine and let it reduce by half. Add the dried shiitake, kombu and double cream and cook over a low heat for 45 minutes. Strain through a chinois and season with lemon juice and salt. In a saucepan, while it's still hot, create foam with a stick blender.

**Serve**
Assemble the onion layers with 1 teaspoon of the corn farofa inside and add 30g of the sea urchin on top. Season with lemon juice and salt. Wrap carefully until everything is all closed inside the onion petals. Arrange in the middle of the bowl and finish by laying 3 tablespoons of the mussel cream around the onion. Garnish with oregano leaves.

—

**Carbon footprint**
double cream 36.28%; sea urchin 16.23%; white wine 11.83%; kombu 8.29%; dried shiitake mushrooms 8.18%; corn farofa 4.85%; onions 4.44%; mussels 3.34%; leek 2.65%; butter 2.58%; olive oil 1.1%; salt 0.84%; lemon juice 0.32%; thyme 0.06%; oregano 0.01%
**Total emissions per serving**
0.91kg $CO_2$e

# SCALLOP, FISH MAYONNAISE → p. 215

- 6 tablespoons Fish Mayonnaise (page 146), in a squeezy bottle
- white Egyptian star cluster flowers, to garnish
- salt, to taste

**For the scallops**
- 100g fine sea salt
- 1kg water
- 11 large scallops

**For the dried scallops**
- 200g shucked scallops
- fine sea salt, to taste

**Scallops**
Dissolve the fine salt in the water in a 10cm-deep 1/3 gastro to make a brine. Shuck the scallops and remove all the guts, then rinse under cold running water to remove any remaining grit or sand. Immerse the scallops in the brine for 8 minutes. Drain the brine, cut each scallop into 4 equal pieces and keep the scallops cool on a paper towel until ready to serve.

**Dried scallops**
Remove all the guts from the shucked scallops, then rinse under cold running water to remove any remaining grit and sand. Place them evenly, side by side, horizontally in a Pacojet beaker and freeze at -18°C (0°F) until solid. Blend, level the surface and freeze again. Repeat 3 times. Put 100g of the scallop mixture between 2 Silpat sheets and roll with a rolling pin until it is evenly spread out and about 1mm thick. Transfer to a 2.5cm-deep 1/1 gastro and refrigerate or freeze for 20 minutes, so you can remove the top Silpat sheet without damaging the surface of the scallop mix. Sprinkle fine sea salt evenly on top and bake in a dry oven with no fan at 100°C (212°F) for 1 hour 10 minutes. Let it cool at room temperature, then break into large pieces and reserve in a sealed container.

**Serve**
Place 7 scallop pieces around the plate and sprinkle salt flakes on top of each scallop. Add drops of the fish mayonnaise between the scallops. Finish with the dried scallop pieces and garnish with the Egyptian star cluster flowers.

—

**Carbon footprint**
scallops 65.81%; salt 28.2%; fish mayonnaise 5.57%; water 0.26%; white Egyptian star cluster flowers 0.16%
**Total emissions per serving**
0.68kg $CO_2e$

# DUCK HEART, BEETROOT CREAM → p. 220

- purple wood sorrel, to garnish
- mini kale leaves, to garnish

**For the duck heart**
- 9 duck hearts, at room temperature
- salt, to taste

**For the beetroot cream**
- 400g red beetroot
- 800g beetroot juice, extracted in a juicer
- lemon juice, to taste
- salt, to taste

**Duck heart**
Sprinkle the duck hearts with salt, then sear them over hot embers for 1 minute on each side. Remove and leave to rest for 2 minutes, then halve through the middle and reserve.

**Beetroot cream**
Preheat the oven to 150°C (302°F). Wrap the red beetroot individually in foil and bake in the oven for 2 hours. Remove from the oven, then leave to cool, peel, and cut into 3cm cubes. Reduce the beetroot juice by half in a saucepan. Add the beetroot cubes to the saucepan and cook over a low heat for 1 hour. Blend in a Thermomix, on high speed, until smooth. Season with lemon juice and salt.

**Serve**
Put three duck heart halves on the right side of the plate, and, on the other side, place 1 tablespoon of the beetroot cream. Garnish with the purple wood sorrel and mini kale leaves around the hearts.

—

**Carbon footprint**
duck hearts 51.22%; beetroot juice 22.06%; salt 11.97%; red beetroot 11.03%; lemon juice 1.43%; purple wood sorrel 1.39%; mini kale leaves 0.9%
**Total emissions per serving**
0.26kg $CO_2$e

# CASHEW CREAM, COCONUT FOAM, TROUT ROE → p. 218

- 180g Raw Cashew Nut Cream (page 144), in a squeezy bottle
- 60g trout roe (the best quality you could get)
- elderflowers, to garnish

**For the coconut foam**

- 1.5kg fresh coconut meat (peel away the outer skin as much as possible), coarsely grated
- lemon juice, to taste
- salt, to taste

**Coconut foam**

Blend the fresh coconut meat in a Thermomix at high speed for 1 minute, until it forms a smooth paste. Strain through a muslin-lined chinois to extract the cream (thicker than the average coconut milk) and season the cream to taste with lemon juice and salt. Heat the coconut milk in a saucepan until lukewarm and froth it with a stick blender.

**Serve**

Put 30g of the raw cashew nut cream at the bottom of a bowl and, right on top, add the trout roe. Lay the foam gently around the roe and garnish with the elderflowers.

—

**Carbon footprint**

raw cashew nut cream 36.14%; coconut 34.73%; trout roe 25.39%; salt 3.21%; lemon juice 0.43%; elderflowers 0.1%

**Total emissions per serving**

0.59kg $CO_2e$

# BRIOCHE, SARDINE, FOIE GRAS → p. 213

- 6 slices (6 x 3cm) of brioche, or any soft bread
- butter, for toasting the brioche
- 6 slices (about 30g each) raw foie gras (out of the main lobe, to avoid any big veins)
- Juniper Powder (page 147), for sprinkling
- salt, to taste

**For the cured sardines**
- 200g salt
- 150g sugar
- grated zest of 1 lemon
- 3 sardines, cleaned and filleted

**For the pickled sardines**
- 100g water
- 100g white vinegar
- 20g salt
- 10g sugar
- 6 cured sardine fillets (see above)

**Cured sardines**
Combine the salt, sugar and lemon zest in a bowl and coat the sardine fillets with the mixture. Let them cure in the refrigerator for 2 hours, then rinse the fillets under cold running water and remove all the fish bones and the skin.

**Pickled sardines**
Combine the water, white vinegar, salt and sugar in a bowl and whisk until the salt and sugar have dissolved. Immerse the cured sardines, then put the pickle solution and the sardines in a vacuum bag and seal under full vacuum. Chill in the refrigerator for 30 minutes.

**Finish**
While the sardines are in the pickle mixture, toast the brioche on both sides in a hot frying pan with 1 tablespoon of butter. Season the foie gras with salt and a pinch of juniper powder. Cut the sardines slightly larger and wider than the brioche and, with a very sharp knife, make parallel incisions along the fillets at a 45-degree angle to a depth of 3mm, each incision spaced 3mm apart.

**Serve**
Assemble the dish on a service tray with the brioche at the base, the foie gras on top, and the cured sardine last. Serve on a napkin folded on a medium plate.

—

**Carbon footprint**
foie gras 33.89%; salt 32.01%; sardines 15.33%; sugar 12.47%; brioche 3.37%; white vinegar 2%; butter 0.9%; lemon zest 0.02%; water 0.01%; juniper powder 0.01%
**Total emissions per serving**
1.29kg $CO_2e$

# BRAZIL NUT ICE CREAM → p. 225

- 6 teaspoons thinly sliced Brazil nuts

**For the Brazil nut ice cream**
- 600g raw Brazil nuts
- 600g Brazil Nut Milk (page 144)
- 90g liquid glucose
- 17g salt
- 600g ice cubes

**Brazil nut ice cream**
Blanch the raw Brazil nuts four times, then drain and blend in a Thermomix at high speed for 30 minutes with the nut milk, glucose and salt. Add the ice and blend for another 5 minutes. Strain through a chinois, pour into a Pacojet beaker and freeze at -18°C (0°F). Spin once before serving.

**Serve**
Place 1 teaspoon of the sliced Brazil nuts in a deep plate and arrange a quenelle of Brazil nut ice cream right on top.

—

**Carbon footprint**
raw Brazil nuts 61.95%; Brazil nut milk 28.73%; thinly sliced Brazil nut 4.34%; liquid glucose 3.18%; salt 1.74%; ice 0.06%
**Total emissions per serving**
1.84kg $CO_2e$

# SNAPPER, KALE, HEART OF PALM, PUMPKIN SEED → p. 209

**For the heart of palm**
- 120g fresh heart of palm
- 30g olive oil, plus extra for drizzling
- 1.2g salt, to taste

**For the pumpkin seed cream**
- 1kg pumpkin seeds
- 60g lemon juice
- 45g ginger juice, extracted in juicer
- 225g Vegetable Base (page 145)
- salt, to taste

**For the bigeye snapper**
- 100g fine sea salt, plus extra to taste
- 1kg water
- 420g bigeye snapper fillets (6 portions of 70g)
- 300g Fish Base (page 145)
- 300g Vegetable Base (page 145)
- olive oil, for brushing

**For the charred kale**
- 12 kale leaves, stems removed
- olive oil, for drizzling
- salt, to taste

**Heart of palm**
Combine the heart of palm with the olive oil and salt in a vacuum bag, seal under full vacuum and cook in a water bath at 100°C (212°F) for 45 minutes or until tender. Remove from the bag, cut into small 5mm cubes and sear in a frying pan over a high heat with a drizzle of olive oil until browned on all sides.

**Pumpkin seed cream**
Grind the pumpkin seeds in a melanger for 12 hours, until the paste has a smooth and consistent texture. Whisk 350g of the paste (you can freeze the rest to use in another recipe) in a bowl with the lemon and ginger juices and vegetable base (cold or at room temperature) and season with salt to taste.

**Bigeye snapper**
Dissolve the fine salt in the water in a 10cm-deep 1/3 gastro to make a brine, then immerse the bigeye snapper fillets in the brine for 8 minutes. Combine the fish and vegetable bases in a saucepan and reduce to a thin glaze. Drain the brine, dry the fillets with a paper towel, then brush them with olive oil, and cook them over hot embers for 2 minutes, turning them frequently to prevent them from burning. Once cooked, brush the glaze on the skin and return to the embers, skin side down for 10 seconds, to caramelize.

**Charred kale**
Season the leaves with a drizzle of olive oil and salt, then char them over hot embers for 30 seconds.

**Serve**
Place 2 tablespoons of the pumpkin seed cream in the middle of the plate, assemble 2 charred kale leaves on top, and cover with 1 tablespoon of the cubed heart of palm. Finish with the bigeye snapper, skin side up.

—

**Carbon footprint**
pumpkin seeds 47.19%; bigeye snapper fillets 14.96%; salt 12.95%; heart of palm 11.48%; vegetable base 5.88%; olive oil 3.51%; fish base 2.55%; ginger juice 0.62%; lemon juice 0.46%; kale 0.29%; water 0.11%
**Total emissions per serving**
1.64kg $CO_2$e

# AÇAÍ SORBET, RAPADURA CRUMBS → p. 223

**For the glucose syrup**
- 1.15kg water
- 475g liquid glucose
- 300g sugar

**For the açaí sorbet**
- 500g açaí pulp
- 100g glucose syrup (above)
- 200g Simple Syrup (page 146)
- 30g lemon juice
- 30g maltodextrin

**For the milk crisp**
- 1kg whole milk
- 200g sugar
- 100g whole milk powder
- 2g salt
- 8g iota carrageenan

**For the açaí crisp**
- 35g sweet cassava starch (tapioca starch)
- 500g açaí pulp
- 50g sugar

**For the rapadura crumbs**
- 100g rapadura
- 100g ground almonds
- 100g cocoa powder

**Glucose syrup**
Put all the ingredients in a saucepan and bring to the boil over a medium heat to dissolve the sugar. Remove from the heat and let it cool at room temperature.

**Açaí sorbet**
Put all the ingredients in a Thermomix and blend at high speed for at least 10 minutes, until smooth. Pour into a Pacojet beaker and freeze at -18°C (0°F). Spin once before serving.

**Milk crisp**
Combine all the ingredients in a Thermomix and blend at high speed until it reaches 70°C (158°F). Transfer the mixture to the bowl of a stand mixer fitted with a whisk attachment and mix at medium speed until it cools to room temperature – the mixture will become porridge-like in texture. Spread the mixture out on a Silpat with a spatula as thinly as possible and dehydrate in a dehydrator at 60°C (140°F) for 2 days. Break into large pieces and reserve in a sealed container.

**Açaí crisp**
Dissolve the sweet cassava in 166g (one-third) of the açaí pulp. Put the sugar and the remaining açaí pulp in a saucepan with the cassava-thickened açaí pulp and cook over a low heat for 5 minutes until it boils, whisking continuously, until the mixture has an elastic-like texture. Pour the mixture over a Silpat and spread it out with a spatula as thinly as possible. Dehydrate in a dehydrator at 60°C (140°F) for 24 hours. Break into large pieces and reserve in a sealed container.

**Rapadura crumbs**
Preheat the oven to 100°C (212°F). Finely grate the rapadura, mix it with the ground almonds and cocoa powder and roast in a shallow gastropan for 1 hour. Let the mixture cool to room temperature, then blend in the Thermomix at high speed until crumbs form.

**Serve**
Place 1 teaspoon of rapadura crumbs in the middle of the plate and shape a quenelle of açaí sorbet on top. Finish with 2 açaí crisps, alternating with the milk crisp.

—

**Carbon footprint**
whole milk 27.03%; sugar 18.17%; açaí 24.82%; liquid glucose 12.25%; cocoa powder 6.92%; simple syrup 3.7%; rapadura 2.89%; whole milk powder 1.66%; ground almonds 1.15%; maltodextrin 0.88%; iota carrageenan 0.24%; lemon juice 0.12%; sweet cassava starch 0.1%; water 0.06%; salt 0.01%
**Total emissions per serving**
3.05kg $CO_2e$

# NOTES ON THE RECIPES

- All recipes (except the base recipes in the Blocks chapter) serve six people.
- All eggs are medium size.
- Certain recipes include eggs, meat and fish that are lightly cooked – these should be avoided by the elderly, infants, pregnant women, individuals recovering from illness, and anyone with a weakened immune system.
- All salt used is salt flakes, unless specified.
- All the eggs used are free range eggs.
- All butter is unsalted.
- Brazilian sugar is similar to European caster sugar.
- All spoon measurements are level. 1 teaspoon = 5ml. 1 tablespoon = 15ml.
- Australian standard tablespoons are 20ml – Australian readers are advised to use 3 teaspoons in place of 1 tablespoon.
- Many of the recipes demand advanced skills, specialized equipment and professional expertise to obtain optimal results.

**The following indigenous ingredients appear in recipes throughout this book:**

**Açaí:** traditionally eaten in savoury preparations in the Amazon, this purple berry is earthy and rich, often blended or served chilled with fish or tapioca.

**Acerola:** bright red and packed with vitamin C, this tart little fruit lends sharp, citrusy intensity to juices, jams and sauces.

**Corn farofa:** this crunchy side dish made from toasted corn flour is a staple on Brazilian tables, perfect for adding texture and soaking up sauces.

**Corn flocão:** pre-cooked, flaked corn used for quick preparations like couscous or cakes, flocão brings the rustic sweetness of corn in a convenient form.

**Jussara:** a native palm fruit similar to açaí, jussara has a deep, winey flavour and connects cuisine with Atlantic Forest conservation.

**Pimenta biquinho:** a mild, pickled pepper shaped like a tiny beak ("biquinho"), it adds a sweet-tangy pop to everything from meats to salads.

**Pimenta de cheiro:** fragrant rather than fiery, these small, colourful peppers bring perfume and complexity to countless Brazilian dishes.

**Pirão:** a comforting porridge made by whisking cassava flour into fish or meat broth, pirão is soulful and rich, traditionally served alongside stews.

**Rapadura:** unrefined sugarcane, pressed and boiled into blocks, rapadura offers earthy sweetness, with subtle notes of caramel and molasses.

**Tucupi:** a bright yellow broth extracted from wild cassava root, tucupi is fermented and then cooked for hours, bringing depth, acidity, and a touch of the Amazon to any dish.

Don Julio
BELVEDERE
VODKA
Havana Club
7
BULLDOG
EMPIRICAL

Maker's Mark

OTEQUE

# INDEX

Page numbers in *italic* refer to the photographs

# B

# D

# I

# L



# M



# O



# P

# R



# S



# T

# V

MICHELIN
2025

For this book to exist, the restaurant had to exist first. I couldn't finish this manuscript without thanking some very special people. To José Roberto Marinho, my business partner, for trusting and supporting the project through both good times and the difficult ones. From the bottom of my heart, thank you for your kindness and generosity.

To two very special families, each generous in their own way: the Tiefel dos Passos family, for all their support when I first arrived in Rio; and the Kawashima family – especially Regina – for opening the door to Japan as I know it today, and for helping me discover so much, with still more to come.

To Andrea Petrini and Robert Astley-Sparke, for leaping into this project with me and pouring your hearts and souls into it. I can never thank you enough for this partnership. And to Flávia too, for the beautiful book design.

To Igor Dinau, my loyal chef, for the many years at my side, for helping with the pictures and recipes, and for caring so deeply for Oteque whenever I had to step away for personal or professional reasons.

To my friends who have travelled the world with me, sharing meals and insights that have made me a better chef and a better person. Forgive me if I forget anyone, but I especially thank Ivan Marchetti, Danilo Nakamura, Renato Tomioka, Arthur Carvalho, Mariano Steinert, Ricardo Carvalho Valente, Pedro Davies, Thiago Pacheco, Marcelo Lorenzen and Maria Mendes.

This year marks my 25th as a chef. Over the years, countless people have crossed my path, and I will inevitably fail to name everyone. But if you were part of this journey, please know how grateful I am – this book belongs to you as well.

Phaidon Press Limited
2 Cooperage Yard
London E15 2QR

Phaidon Press Inc.
111 Broadway
New York, NY 10006

Phaidon SARL
55, rue Traversière
75012 Paris

phaidon.com

First published 2026


ISBN 978 1 83729 062 8
ISBN 978 1 83729 252 3 (signed edition)

A CIP catalogue record for this book is available from the British Library and the Library of Congress.



Commissioning Editor: Emilia Terragni
Project Editor: Laura Nicholl
Production Controller: Adela Cory
Photography: Robert Astley-Sparke
Design: Flávia Nalon/ps.2

Printed in China

Phaidon would like to thank Hilary Bird, Adela Cory, João Mota, Faye Robinson, Clare Rogers, Ellie Smith and Tracey Smith.